PRIMARY SOURCES

FOR

VICTORIAN STUDIES

A Guide to the Location and Use of
Unpublished Materials

by

RICHARD STOREY

and

LIONEL MADDEN

PHILLIMORE

1977

Published by PHILLIMORE & CO., LTD.,
London and Chichester

Head Office: Shopwyke Hall,
Chichester, Sussex, England

ISBN 0 85033 252 4

Text set in 11/12pt. Baskerville

Printed in Great Britain by
Unwin Brothers, Ltd., Old Woking, Surrey

CONTENTS

PREFACE

THIS SHORT GUIDE has been written primarily to assist students who are commencing research projects within the scope of what are now generally known as Victorian Studies. (The chronological limits are obviously not restricted rigidly to the period 1837-1901.) It attempts to provide a concise elementary statement of basic information about the location and use of manuscripts and other unpublished source materials with which all such students should become familiar as soon as possible after commencing their research. The guide concentrates on collections within Britain, but a short section is included as an introduction to the problems of discovering collections of relevant materials outside Britain. Bibliographical references are included throughout the text.

This guide is, of course, based on the professional experience of its authors and the exchange of ideas with colleagues. The views expressed, however, are those of the authors themselves and should not be taken to represent the official views of any organisation with which they are or have been associated.

Acknowledgement is made to the Governors of New College, London, for permission to quote from the letters of Dr. John Pye Smith.

NOTE

Full bibliographical details of all publications are included in the text. Place of publication for books is London unless otherwise stated. Every effort has been made to up-date information to 1975 with a few later references.

THE RESEARCH STUDENT AND HIS MATERIALS

> On the eastern borders of Chancery Lane, that is to say,
> more particularly in Cook's Court, Cursitor Street, Mr.
> Snagsby, Law-Stationer, pursues his lawful calling. In the
> shade of Cook's Court, at most times a shady place, Mr.
> Snagsby has dealt in all sorts of blank forms of legal process;
> in skins and rolls of parchment; in paper — foolscap, brief,
> draft, brown, white, whitey-brown, and blotting; in stamps;
> in office-quills, pens, ink, India-rubber, pounce, pins, pencils,
> sealing-wax, and wafers; in red tape and green ferret; in
> pocket-books, almanacks, diaries, and law lists; in string
> boxes, rulers, inkstands—glass and leaden, penknives, scissors,
> bodkins, and other small office-cutlery; in short, in articles
> too numerous to mention; ever since he was out of his time,
> and went into partnership with Peffer.

Dickens's account of the contents of Mr. Snagsby's shop in
Bleak House provides an evocative description of some of the
19th-century office materials which have provided the raw
materials of research for 20th-century students. The student
of 19th-century Britain, indeed, is confronted by a remarkable
amount of unpublished source materials. The enormous output
of manuscripts and documents during this period may be
attributed to several social and economic causes. In an age
which preceded the widespread use of the telephone the normal
method of private and official communication was still the
written word. As the century progressed the habit of writing
letters and exchanging documents received encouragement
from the growing efficiency of both the postal service and the
railways, and from the spread of basic literacy. New cheap
methods of manufacturing paper, which contributed to the
rapid growth of the periodical and newspaper press, also
encouraged the production of both private and official letters
and documents.

Although the output of manuscripts and documents thus
became larger and more varied than in any previous age, the

general lack of any very effective copying techniques restricted the number of copies which could be produced by offices. This inhibited such developments as the modern habit of issuing duplicated circulars, although printing was to some extent an economically feasible substitute. For the same reason exchanges of official documents and correspondence tended to be limited to the principals involved. Surprisingly little, in fact, is known about the details of office practice in the 19th century. The Science Museum (Exhibition Road, South Kensington, London, S.W.7) has on display a permanent exhibit of typewriters and other examples of office equipment. The examples of typewriters in the Science Museum are well documented in *The History and Development of Typewriters,* by G. Tilghman Richards, revised by W. E. Church (2nd ed., H.M.S.O., 1964).[1] In fact, however, typewriters do not seem to have become commercially popular in the United Kingdom until the last decade of the 19th century. Throughout most of the century office clerks used pens and wrote documents and letters by hand. An anonymous study of 'The use of quill, patent and steel pens by the Bank of England during the nineteenth century'[2] reveals that in 1810 each clerk was using approximately five quill pens every working day. Although the Bank of England later changed to the Bramah patent pen and then to steel nibs, purchases of quill pens continued as late as 1907.

In *The Origin of Stencil Duplicating* (Hutchinson, 1972)[3] W. B. Proudfoot traces the evolution of copying techniques and emphasises the revolutionary effect of the invention of the stencil process during the last quarter of the 19th century. During the first half of the century copies were made, if at all, by copy clerks who simply re-wrote the documents and letters. Later in the century—probably about 1875— the letter-copying book was widely adopted in offices. The copying book consisted of tissues, each of which, when dampened, would take under pressure a copy from a recently-written original. Although the impression formed a mirror-image of the original the text could be read through the tissue.

Despite the relative wealth of source materials produced in the 19th century the student encounters other difficulties in discovering precisely what exists and where it is located.

The lapse of time, which makes 19th-century materials more readily available for research than more recent documents, also makes them often difficult to trace. The World Wars were responsible not only for the destruction of much material but also for the widespread scattering of manuscripts and records. The modern researcher is thus faced with a paradoxical situation in which, although large numbers of documents still survive, their elusiveness makes it difficult for him to trace and use them effectively.

The type of problem commonly encountered by students may be readily illustrated by the difficulties which often arise in locating and using 19th-century correspondence. The letters of most correspondents can be traced only by an examination of the surviving archives of all those to whom they wrote. Some individuals, of course, retained files of letters received and copies of letters sent. Frequently, however, the hobby of collecting autographs encouraged the fragmentation of archives. Many individual letters of prominent Victorians have entered, and are still entering, the autograph market, and by no means all of them can safely be assumed to be relatively unimportant social letters concerning invitations and the like. Even if single letters enter the collections of repositories, the problem of circulating information about their existence remains considerable. The listing of such letters without any indication of their subject contents, although an unsatisfactory expedient, often has to be resorted to for reasons of time and expense. Even if a list is made by the repository, this may well remain merely as a card index within the repository, making it very difficult for the research student to track down. The problem of locating such items of correspondence is still further complicated by the continued existence of much material in private hands.

While the seriousness of such difficulties is real and should certainly not be underestimated, it is evident that the adoption of a sensible and systematic approach to the search for original materials will considerably increase the effectiveness of the student's research. Many students still receive little or no formal instruction in the techniques of such an investigation. The present work is arranged in two parts, dealing with the two aspects of any search for source materials. The first, and major, part attempts to provide a brief introduction to the problems and offers some suggestions for a systematic search which will help to reduce wastage of time and effort. This part is concerned mainly with the discovery of source materials in Britain, but it also includes some hints on the location of overseas sources. It does not aim to provide a checklist of the sources themselves—though the scope of several of these is indicated incidentally—but a guide to the major sources of information about archives. The second part of the guide offers a brief introduction to the use of source materials. It provides information about the specialised methods of arrangement employed by archivists and other keepers of materials, and gives some elementary practical hints for students using such materials, as well as an introduction to the terminology likely to be encountered.

THE HISTORICAL MANUSCRIPTS COMMISSION AND
THE NATIONAL REGISTER OF ARCHIVES

Introductory

It is the ideal of every student to find a single comprehensive guide to all the source materials relevant to his own and related fields of research. Inevitably, if unfortunately, no such guide generally exists. In the course of most research projects the student must undertake a painstaking search through the information contained in general guides, the indexes of major collections, and the holdings of any collections which have a special interest in his own subject field. The following chapters offer guidance in this search for information.

The Historical Manuscripts Commission

The establishment of a Royal Commission for locating and publishing manuscripts and papers of institutions and private families 'for the elucidation of History, and the illustration of Constitutional Law, Science and Literature' was an essentially Victorian way of approaching the problem (and opportunities) presented by non-governmental manuscripts. The Commission was established by Royal Warrant in 1869. Its centenary year, 1969, was marked by an exhibition at the National Portrait Gallery, for which a definitive illustrated catalogue, *Manuscripts and Men* (H.M.S.O., 1969), was produced. This included a historical account of the Commission by its Secretary. A number of articles on the Commission's history and current activities was also published.[1]

For many years the work of the Historical Manuscripts Commission was synonymous with a series of printed *Reports* and *Appendices* in which were published both summary descriptions of the archives of noble families, private persons, and ancient institutions, and detailed calendars of sections of these. This series of publications has little to offer the student of the 19th century, since 19th-century manuscripts were generally regarded by the Commission and its inspectors as current records, and hence do not feature in the *Reports*. Today the Commission is still a publishing body, but during the last quarter of a century its activities have broadened considerably and are now of great relevance and value for 19th-century studies. Full details of the Commission's publications may be found in *Sectional List No. 17: Publications of the Royal Commission on Historical Manuscripts,* which is issued free by H.M.S.O.

In the field of publishing, the most important development has been the inauguration of a new series to publish selected portions of the private and personal papers of 19th-century prime ministers. Mr. John Brooke was appointed senior editor of this series in 1964 and the first volume, a survey entitled *The Prime Ministers' Papers 1801–1902,* was published by H.M.S.O. in 1968. Statements of the senior editor's publication policy will be found both in the introduction to this volume and in a memorandum published as Appendix I to the 25th *Report to the Crown* (H.M.S.O., 1967). The first texts to be published are Gladstone's *Autobiographica* (H.M.S.O., 1972), and *Autobiographical Memoranda* (H.M.S.O., 1973).

Another innovation is the Joint Publications series, first described in the 23rd *Report to the Crown* (H.M.S.O., 1961), by which the Commission assists record societies with the publication of volumes which they would not be able to issue on the strength of their own resources. One 19th-century work assisted in this way is JP3, *John Constable's Correspondence: The Family at East Bergholt 1807–1837* (H.M.S.O., 1962), the first of a series being continued by the Suffolk Records Society. Another source in preparation is the Board Minutes, 1845–52, of the Reading, Guildford & Reigate Railway.

The Historical Manuscripts Commission's increased activity in the sphere of scientific manuscripts in recent years— especially through its Standing Joint Committee with the Royal Society—is indicated by the preparation for publication of a *Guide* to scientists' papers. This has been edited by

Dr. R. E. W. Maddison and W. J. Craig, though it is not yet published. The *Guide* will cover the period from the 16th century to the time of Lord Rutherford and will inevitably contain information about much 19th-century material.

Other publications of the Commission include an annual *Accessions to Repositories and Reports Added to the National Register of Archives* (H.M.S.O.)[2] which gives summary details of major accessions received by principal repositories during the year prior to publication. Many of these accessions may not be listed in detail for a number of years after the appearance of *Accessions to Repositories*. The Commission also publishes a guide to *Record Repositories in Great Britain*. This basic directory of repositories is revised every few years. The most recent edition is the fifth, published by H.M.S.O. late in 1973 (reprinted with addenda, pp. 66-7, 1976). The sixth edition will be the first to incorporate the effects of the 1974 local government changes.

The National Register of Archives ·

The other major aspect of the post-war broadening of the Historical Manuscripts Commission's activities is the maintenance of the National Register of Archives, which was established in 1945 under the aegis of the Commission to carry out a survey of the location of private papers, following the disruption which it was feared had been caused by the Second World War. The usefulness of the Register's findings led to its development as a permanent part of the Commission's activities, operated by the Commission's staff and now fully integrated into the whole work of the Historical Manuscripts Commission. The National Register of Archives fulfils its role as a centralised information centre on non-governmental records by the collection and indexing of lists (N.R.A. reports) from repositories throughout the country and others produced by its own staff. The holdings of the National Register exceeded 19,000 lists in 1975. Approximately 1,000 new reports, as well as numerous and sometimes large additions to existing ones, are filed each year. New reports are listed in *Accessions to Repositories,* continuing the numerically-arranged listing begun in the *Report of the Secretary* (1969). The reports are indexed in detail by subjects and by personal names, the latter in computer print-out form. In general only persons of sufficient eminence to appear in the *Dictionary of National Biography* or *Who Was Who* are indexed. The reports are also indexed selectively for places: most references to overseas places are indexed; within the United Kingdom index entries emphasise 'out-county' material, such as Essex estate papers now located in Devon. There is also a central index to the archives for which lists are held, and there are locational and partial numerical indexes which may be consulted on application to the staff. An article by R. A. Storey on 'Indexing archives' in *The Indexer*[3] gives some indication of the practice followed by the National Register in the 1960s.

The lists held by the National Register vary in character according to the practice of the issuing repository. A number consist of a single folio (a first-stage report) giving simply the barest details of an archive and its location. The other extreme is represented by such lists as that made by the Commission's staff of the extensive correspondence of Frederick Locker-Lampson, the Victorian writer of *vers de société*, in which each item is individually described. This Locker-Lampson archive group is now deposited in the East Sussex Record Office.[4]

The Commission's staff has produced only a small percentage of the lists added in each year, but these include lists of national significance, such as: the correspondence of Lord Palmerston (Broadlands Archive); the archives of New College, London, with abundant details of local Congregationalism in the first half of the 19th century, as well as material on the College and its predecessors and on 19th-century nonconformity in general; and the deposited manuscripts at the Royal Institute of British Architects, which are rich in 19th-century material. Work is currently in progress on the sorting, prior to listing, of some 40,000 letters received by Oscar Browning, which had remained uncatalogued for several decades at Hastings Public Library. The papers of Field Marshal Lord Wolseley in Hove Central Library and the Royal United Service Institution have also been listed in recent years, the latter at short notice to facilitate their transfer to Hove.

The preceding paragraph indicates only a selection of the more important 19th-century sources listed by the Commission's staff in the 1960s and early 1970s. Further details will be found in the *Bulletin of the National Register of Archives,* published by H.M.S.O. between 1948 and 1967, and in the new annual *Report of the Secretary to the Commissioners* (later re-titled *Secretary's Report to the Commissioners*). The first *Report,* for 1968-69, was published by H.M.S.O. in 1969. The preponderance of 19th-century papers dealt with by the Commission in recent years probably reflects the relative abundance of manuscripts surviving from this period. The researcher can reasonably hope that much more still remains to be discovered and listed.

Copies of the lists reproduced by the Commission and filed in the National Register are sent to the copyright libraries and to a number of other national institutions. Copies of those with a particular local interest are also sent to the repositories concerned. The only complete set, however, is held in the National Register of Archives itself, where it may be used in conjunction with the unique indexes. In order to make some of the information in the National Register more widely available, a series of source guides has been developed. These note references to relevant materials which are found in the lists held in the National Register. *Sources of Business History in the National Register of Archives* appeared annually from 1964 to 1972, while *Architectural History and the Fine and Applied Arts: Sources in the National Register of Archives* commenced publication in 1969. Each list is arranged in a single alphabetical sequence of names. A brief summary of the nature of the material is given, together with the N.R.A. report number. For further information and the location of the material the student must consult the reports in the National Register's search room. Details of the prices of the duplicated source lists can be obtained from the Commission. Plans are in hand for the preparation of a more substantive series of *Guides to Sources for British History.*[5]

No reader's ticket is necessary to use the search room in the National Register of Archives, which is open during normal office hours, Monday to Friday. The full postal address is: Historical Manuscripts Commission, Quality House, Quality Court, Chancery Lane, London, WC2A 1HP. The nearest underground stations are Chancery Lane (Central) and Temple

(Circle and District). Although limited enquiries can be answered by post, a personal visit to the National Register is always recommended. A set of descriptive leaflets on the Commission, its publications, the National Register of Archives, and the Manorial Documents Register, is available without charge from the Commission's office.

NATIONAL REPOSITORIES

THE SIZE and complexity of the holdings of the national repositories make them difficult subjects for description within the compass of a short guide. However, some general points can be made, particularly with reference to the existence of printed lists and catalogues.

Public Records

Most, but not all, of the records of the central government and its activities are housed in the Public Record Office (Chancery Lane, London, WC2A 1LR). Work is now advanced on a new building at Kew to which will be transferred the bulk of the modern records.[1] The existing office in Chancery Lane will continue to house medieval records and State papers, including those records described in volume one of the *Guide*.

The main holdings of the Public Record Office to 1960 are summarised in the *Guide to the Contents of the Public Record Office* (3 vols., H.M.S.O., 1963–8) and in supplementary volumes, such as *Maps and Plans in the Public Record Office, pt. I: British Isles, c. 1410–1860* (H.M.S.O., 1967), and the *Handbook* series. The *Guide* is an essential starting point for any research on the public records. Important new accessions are noted in the annual *Report of the Keeper of Public Records* (H.M.S.O.). The office also issues a guide to *Record Publications* (H.M.S.O.) which lists public records and guides which have been published. In 1965 a List and Index Society was formed to distribute to members bound copies of unpublished Public Record Office search room lists and indexes.

In addition to its main holdings the Public Record Office also contains some deposited material; these deposits are usually listed only in brief handlists. The Scottish Record

Office, which is the Scottish equivalent of the Public Record Office, is notable for its extensive holdings of private papers, there being no local network of county record offices as in England. The first volume of the *List of Gifts and Deposits in the Scottish Record Office* (Edinburgh, H.M.S.O., 1971) records mainly family muniments, but also indicates some business archives and miscellaneous deposits. The older guides to the Scottish Record Office are now in process of revision, but brief source lists are available.

When using public records it should be remembered that in the 19th century such records were more likely to pass out of official custody into the archives of retiring ministers than they are today. Such *semi-official* papers must therefore generally be sought amongst private papers, for example, Lord Palmerston's correspondence in the Broadlands Archive.[2]

The records of some aspects of central government or State activity are held in separate repositories, for example, the India Office Records and Library (see Chapter 7), the Customs and Excise Records, and the records of what was formerly the General Post Office (Post Office Records, St. Martin's-le-Grand, London, E.C.1; related material is held in the National Postal Museum, King Edward Building, King Edward Street, London, E.C.1, including the De La Rue stamp-printing archive: see p. 76, note 30).

Nationalised Industries

With the exception of the National Coal Board, the Post Office (formerly the General Post Office), and the United Kingdom Atomic Energy Authority, the records of the nationalised industries—most of which have their origins in the technological developments of the 19th century—are not classed as public records and so will not be found in the Public Record Office.[3] The National Coal Board, in fact, has its own archive organisation, and so have the Post Office and the British Steel Corporation, the latter only established in 1970. Scottish railway records were transferred to the Scottish Record Office in 1970 and there are plans for the British Rail archives to be housed in the Public Record Office buildings at Kew, the archive which the British Transport Commission had set up being administered by the Public Record Office from April 1972.[4] The records of many *local* gas companies and those of some electricity power companies are to be found in local record offices where they have been deposited by area boards.

Parliamentary Records

The records of the legislature, as opposed to those of the executive, are housed in the House of Lords Record Office, which was established as recently as 1946 to concentrate and care for the scattered records of Parliament. In 1970 a 30-year access rule was introduced to apply to the records of the House of Commons, thereby releasing a vast quantity of historical sources. The records of the House of Lords, as a 'court of record', had always been generally available. In 1971 a clear and comprehensive *Guide to the Records of Parliament,* by Maurice Bond, the Clerk of the Records, was published by H.M.S.O.[5] This is a model of its kind, describing the voluminous records of both Houses, class by class, with a list of the classes preceding each main section, and with a detailed index. It is impossible to single out any particular class for comment. Some, such as the Private Bill records, are already familiar, for example to transport historians, for the Railway Bills they contain. Perhaps less familiar are some of the Historical Collections, which include a number of unexpected deposits, such as that of the Commons and Footpaths Preservation Society, a typical mid-Victorian public-spirited endeavour. More familiar or expected are such deposits as the Hardman drawings by Pugin and others for the new Houses of Parliament, 1835–55, and the diaries and correspondence of Speaker Brand. It should also be noted that a deposit such as the Samuel Papers which is primarily associated with the 20th century in fact begins in the last quarter of the 19th century.

Although not strictly a *primary* source, the Irish University Press series of subject sets of *British Parliamentary Papers* is worth mentioning here. The Parliamentary Papers or Blue Books include the *Reports* of Select Committees and Royal Commissions, as well as correspondence and papers ordered by the House to be printed, and total approximately 7,000 volumes. The Irish University Press series groups items relating to the same subject in one or more volumes and provides indexes with critical commentaries for each subject.

Introductory guides to Parliamentary papers and the existing breviates and select lists of 19th-century papers are discussed in John E. Pemberton, *British Official Publications* (2nd ed., Oxford, Pergamon, 1973).

National Library Collections

Within the context of an introductory guide it would be unrealistic to attempt any evaluative comment on the manuscript holdings of the national libraries, except perhaps to underline the regional relevance of the holdings of the National Library of Scotland and the National Library of Wales, for their respective countries, whilst in no way diminishing their significance for British and, indeed, Western culture as a whole. The present work attempts only to indicate the principal published finding-aids for the manuscript holdings of the national libraries. It should, of course, be remembered that their major accessions are recorded from year to year in *Accessions to Repositories* (H.M.S.O.).

BRITISH LIBRARY[6]

Catalogue of Additions to Manuscripts in the British Museum: lists accessions to 1945. The multi-volume *Catalogue* includes *The Gladstone Papers* (1953) and *Plays Submitted to the Lord Chamberlain, 1824–1851* (1964).

Augustus Hughes-Hughes, *Catalogue of Manuscript Music in the British Museum* (3 vols., 1906–9).

T. C. Skeat, *The Catalogues of the Manuscript Collections* (revised edition, 1962).

The British Museum: A Guide to its Public Services (revised edition, 1970).

British Library Journal: a twice-yearly periodical (Spring, 1975 –), which includes information about new accessions. Supersedes *British Museum Quarterly*.

BODLEIAN LIBRARY, OXFORD

F. Madan, H. H. E. Craster, N. Denholm-Young and R. W. Hunt, *A Summary Catalogue of Western Manuscripts in the*

> *Bodleian Library at Oxford* (7 vols. in 8, 1922-53): only lists accessions to 1915.
> *Bodleian Library Record*: twice-yearly. Includes notes on new accessions.
> *Annual Report of the Curators of the Bodleian Library*.

CAMBRIDGE UNIVERSITY LIBRARY

Summary Guide to Accessions of Western Manuscripts (Other than Medieval) since 1867 (1966): the original *Catalogue of the Manuscripts* (5 vols. and index) was published during 1856-67.

Handlists: *Darwin Papers* (1960): papers of Charles Darwin.
     Hardinge Papers (1968): papers of the first Lord Hardinge of Penshurst.

NATIONAL LIBRARY OF SCOTLAND

Catalogue of Manuscripts: 4 vols. published (1938-71), of which Volume III is devoted entirely to the Blackwood Papers (see Chapter 7).

Annual Report: discontinued in 1958 and succeeded by: *Accessions of Manuscripts, 1959-1964, Accessions of Manuscripts 1965-1970*.

NATIONAL LIBRARY OF WALES

Handlist of Manuscripts in the National Library of Wales (1940-).

Annual Report.

Irish Repositories

Much Irish material, such as estate papers, will be found as an integral part of family papers in private hands or deposited in English, Scottish and Welsh repositories. The principal repositories to approach in Ireland are: the Public Record Office of Northern Ireland, Belfast (which, like the Scottish Record Office, has extensive holdings of private papers);[7] the Public Record Office of Ireland (note that the Record Office was destroyed in 1922); the State Paper Office; the National Library of Ireland; Trinity College, Dublin. The last four repositories are all in Dublin. An important guide to manuscript sources is Richard J. Hayes, *Manuscript Sources for the History of Irish Civilization* (11 vols., Boston, Mass., 1966). The publications of the Irish Manuscripts Commission, which include *Analecta Hibernica* with their reports on records, should also be consulted.[8] Particularly noteworthy is the *Guide to Irish Quaker Records 1654-1860,* by Olive C. Goodbody, with a contribution by B. G. Hutton (Dublin, Irish Stationery Office, 1966). Edith M. Johnston's short but useful bibliography, *Irish History: A Select Bibliography* (rev. ed., Historical Association, 1972) should also be consulted.

LOCAL REPOSITORIES

PRIOR TO THE INTRODUCTION of the two-tier system of local government on 1 April 1974, there was a fairly complete network of county record offices in England and Wales. Among the few exceptions the most notable was the West Riding of Yorkshire.[1] The primary task of the county record offices has always been to preserve the records of their respective county councils, instituted in 1888, and their predecessors as judicial and administrative bodies, the Quarter Sessions. Over the years they have also attracted gifts and deposits of private papers, such as the records of estates and families located within their administrative areas. An outstanding example of this is found at Hawarden in Flintshire, where the Flintshire Record Office has taken over the task of listing some 50,000 documents, including all W. E. Gladstone's private correspondence. This material was returned to Hawarden Castle in 1930 when Gladstone's political papers were deposited in the British Museum. Although the private papers have been deposited in the magnificent St. Deiniol's Library in Hawarden, which houses Gladstone's own library, responsibility for listing them has rightly been assumed by the local record office. In fact, some offices have throughout their period of existence been concerned more with such private papers than with the administrative records of their authorities. In some cases (especially in 1973-4) county record offices have received deposits of non-current records from the lower-tier local authorities within their boundaries. These include boroughs, rural and urban districts, civil parishes and their predecessors, such as local boards of health. Virtually every county repository, too, has received as deposits quantities of ecclesiastical records, especially Anglican parish records, often as a result of systematic surveys of such material.

A few county record offices were formerly administered join-
tly as combined county and borough repositories. Examples of
these were Ipswich and East Suffolk, and Bury St. Edmunds
and West Suffolk Record Offices.[2] All county records are
likely to contain much source material for 19th-century studies,
most obviously relating to local government and estate administration, but also to local commercial and manufacturing actvity
and the work of public utility undertakings. They will also
contain sources for the study at local level of what may be
broadly termed social and cultural phenomena. In some cases
the county record offices will also house manuscripts of
national significance.

Examination of the Historical Manuscripts Commission's
Record Repositories in Great Britain (H.M.S.O.) will reveal a
considerable number of published guides to the holdings of
record offices. However, the cumulative effect of those offices
which have no published guides and of guides which are as
much as 20 years old is to produce a serious lack of concise
information about the holdings of record offices as a whole.
This applies especially to holdings of private papers. Since
official records are nominally their basic *raison d'etre* a guide
which is published in parts will usually devote the first volume
to quarter session and county council records. The second
volume, listing other collections, will often be slow to follow.

It would be invidious to select from the published guides
any for special mention but, simply as examples of what the
researcher might hope for, we may cite the Essex *Guide* (1969),
the Kent *Guides* and *Supplement* (1958, 1971, 1972), the
Oxfordshire *Summary Catalogue of Privately Deposited
Records* (1966), the *Guide to Great Yarmouth Borough
Records* (Norfolk and Norwich R.O., 1973), and the area
subject guides produced as a co-operative effort by the Hampshire Archivists' Group: *Poor Law in Hampshire through the
Centuries, a Guide to the Records* and *Transport in Hampshire
and the Isle of Wight, a Guide to the Records* (Winchester,
1970, 1973).

There are several ways in which some of the deficiencies in
printed information can be made good. The detailed annual
reports produced by some offices, notably Lincolnshire, and,
more recently, the North Riding of Yorkshire, can build up

into a useful substitute for a guide to private papers in record offices. An overall picture of recent deposits since the mid-1950s, although lacking in detail, can be obtained from returns published in the Historical Manuscript commission's annual *List of Accessions to Repositories* (H.M.S.O.)[3] which includes contributions from many local and other repositories. In due course many of these accessions are recorded in detailed catalogues filed in the National Register of Archives, as explained in Chapter Two. Essential details of many, but by no means all repositories are given in *Record Repositories in Great Britain* (H.M.S.O.). The principal exclusions from this work are some local repositories maintained without archive staff as part of the library system.

Such local history collections in public libraries may include manuscripts, printed and visual sources. In addition to major public libraries, such as Birmingham and Manchester, some of the smaller ones have very important deposits or collections. Good examples for the 19th century are the John Clare manuscripts at Northampton, listed in *Catalogue of the John Clare Collection in the Northampton Public Library* (Northampton, Public Libraries, Museums and Art Gallery Committee, 1964), and the papers of Field Marshal Lord Wolseley at Hove Public Library, listed by the National Register of Archives (N.R.A. 10471). Museums, too, sometimes house manuscripts. Keats House in Hampstead is an outstanding example of such a collection. Details of the collections in libraries and museums may be found in the directories listed in Chapter Five. Some additional information about museums may be traced in the annual *Museums and Galleries in Great Britain and Ireland* (Dunstable, Index Publishers).

As can be inferred from the foregoing remarks, local archive-keeping is far from comprehensive. In particular, as urban historians discovered, there were too many groups of local authority records (including, of course, also records of rural authorities) lying neglected in town halls and district council offices. The 1974 reorganisation did not necessarily result in the wholesale transfer of records, but the administrative reorganisation undoubtedly brought many neglected records into the care of archive offices.[4]

F. G. Emmison, *Introduction to Archives* (rev. ed., Chichester, Phillimore, 1977) is an invaluable short introductory pamphlet which concentrates especially on local sources. F. G. Emmison and Irvine Gray, *County Records: (Quarter Sessions, Petty Sessions, Clerk of the Peace and Lieutenancy)* (rev. ed., Historical Association, 1961) aims 'to introduce the general reader to the rich sources of material which are found in our Quarter Sessions records and other official archives of the English and Welsh counties'. *Local Records: Their Nature and Care,* edited by L. J. Redstone and F. W. Steer (Bell, for The Society of Archivists, 1953) although written primarily for archivists, includes much useful information for the research student. Further information on the wide range of material which awaits the researcher in local record offices will be found in F. G. Emmison and W. J. Smith, *Material for Theses in Some Local Record Offices* (Chichester, Phillimore, for the British Records Association, 1973). A second revised and expanded edition is in preparation.

Although the study of local materials is obviously pertinent primarily to local historians, many of the works written for them offer useful guidance to students with a wide range of subject interests. Among works for local historians F. G. Emmison, *Archives and Local History* (rev. ed., Chichester, Phillimore, 1972), W. G. Hoskins, *Local History in England* (2nd ed., Longmans, 1972) and *Sources for English Local History*, by W. B. Stephens (Manchester University Press, 1972) are essential reading. J. L. Hobbs, *Local History and the Library* (2nd ed., rev. by George A. Carter, Deutsch, 1973) includes information on both printed and manuscript sources. Alan Rogers, *This Was Their World; Approaches to Local History* (B.B.C., 1972) provides a detailed and very useful guide to the manifold variety of local records, which might be referred to with profit by those researching subjects other than local history, with the proviso that it does not deal with deposits of national significance, such as the papers of literary or political figures which are to be found in some local repositories.

For those who need to cope with deeds relating to property transactions, Julian Cornwall, *How To Read Old Title Deeds* (Birmingham, University Department of Extra-Mural Studies,

1964, reprinted Pinhorns, 1971), will prove useful, especially for transactions prior to the Real Property Act of 1845. The standard guides to wills are Anthony J. Camp, *Wills and Their Whereabouts* (4th ed., privately published, 1974) and J. S. W. Gibson, *Wills and Where to Find Them* (Chichester, Phillimore for British Record Society, 1974). These are, of course, especially useful in the search for wills proved before the establishment in 1858 of the Principal Probate Registry, now located in Somerset House. Several of the leaflets issued by the Historical Association in the series of *Short Guides to Records*, edited by Lionel M. Munby, offer brief guidance for searches in specialised 19th-century records.

GENERAL PUBLISHED GUIDES

Directories

In addition to the general works issued by the Historical Manuscripts Commission and the National Register of Archives and the guides to specific collections of source materials noted in the preceding chapters, there are a few reference works which may offer some assistance to the student at an early stage in his research. The most important general guide to libraries and organisations in Britain as sources of information is the *Aslib Directory*, edited by Brian J. Wilson (2 vols., Aslib, 1968-70). This completely revised and re-arranged edition is based on earlier editions in 1928 and 1957. The first volume, covering science, technology and commerce, will be of little value to students of the 19th century. The second volume, however, 'includes sources of information on medicine, the social sciences and the humanities, including law, history, geography, theology, sport and the arts generally'.[1] Within each volume entries are arranged alphabetically by postal towns. For each institution or organisation details are given of the scope of its interest and the size of its library stock. Where applicable, publications issued by the body are listed as a guide to its authority within its subject field. Each volume includes alphabetical name and subject indexes.

The fundamental problem of using the *Aslib Directory* derives from the fact that its information is based on answers to questionnaires. The previous editor, Miriam Alman, noted that in such answers the librarian of a small collection will justifiably report a special collection in his library which might well pass unnoticed on the shelves of a larger institution. This makes it difficult to draw very valid conclusions about the relative importance of the collections listed within a given subject field and also means that some collections in large libraries may well not be reported. Nevertheless, the *Aslib Directory* is of considerable value in enabling the student to locate collections in less well-known and unexpected libraries and also in indicating organisations and institutions which might be able to offer advice and information about the location of source materials. Obviously, the emphasis in the entries is on collections of books, but there are nevertheless many useful references to manuscript collections, as the following entry indicates:

LINCOLN   TENNYSON RESEARCH CENTRE   *Tel.:* Lincoln 28621
                 Lincoln City Libraries
854   Free School Lane
                 Lincoln

The Research Centre, at the City Libraries, consists of 4,700 books, letters and manuscripts relating to Alfred Lord Tennyson, deposited by the Tennyson family, and the City Library's own Tennyson collection. There is also much illustrative material, tapes, records, proofs and family papers. Written application should be made to work in the Centre

*Publications:*A catalogue is to be published in three parts. This will consist of:

    Part 1. Libraries of members of the Tennyson family.
    Part 2. Books written by and about Alfred Lord
           Tennyson
    Part 3. Manuscript material including letters

Associated with the Research Centre is a Tennyson Exhibition Room at the Usher Gallery (no. 855), where exhibits illustrate the poet's personality, his life and family background, the range and sources of his poetic output and his methods of work

The Tennyson Research Centre is supported in its work by the Tennyson Society and the Tennyson Trust which is a charitable trust receiving grants for the work of cataloguing the material in the Centre. The Society publishes annually the Tennyson Research Bulletin

If this entry demonstrates the value of the *Aslib Directory* in the search for information about collections of unpublished materials, reference to the index entry for Tennyson indicates that, like all general guides, this is inevitably incomplete. The index directs the reader to this entry and to the succeeding entry for the collections in the Usher Gallery in Lincoln, but contains no reference to the extremely important collection of unpublished material in Trinity College, Cambridge.

For the student who is engaged in a preliminary search for source materials the most valuable service provided by the *Aslib Directory* will clearly be to offer suggestions about where to enquire for information. A few other guides may give additional help at this stage. *The Libraries, Museums and Art Galleries Year Book,* edited by Edmund V. Corbett (Cambridge, Clarke, latest edition 1971), which, despite its title is not a regular annual publication, offers concise information on the scope of collections in public, academic and special libraries and in museums and art galleries in the United Kingdom and in Eire. This will sometimes supply information excluded from the *Aslib Directory*. There is a useful short list of catalogues compiled for manuscript holdings in British libraries of all types in a pamphlet by Philip Hepworth, *Archives and Manuscripts in Libraries* (2nd ed., Library Association, 1964).

A very good example of a survey of library collections within a specific geographical location is A. N. L. Munby, *Cambridge College Libraries: Aids for Research Students* (2nd ed., Cambridge, Heffer, 1962). This short guide attempts to draw to the attention of research students special collections of books and manuscripts housed in the college libraries of Cambridge, and in the Fitzwilliam Museum and the University Archives. The choice of collections is determined by their potentialities for research and the guide draws attention to much relatively unknown material, including a number of interesting 19th-century manuscripts. Especially notable are the 19th-century literary manuscripts in Trinity College and the literary and artistic manuscripts in the Fitzwilliam Museum. It should be noted that Munby's work does not include references to the collections of the University Library and the faculty libraries. For these reference should be made to the *Guide to the Libraries of the University of Cambridge* (Cambridge, University Library). A comparable study to Munby's for Oxford was published by the Oxford Bibliographical Society and the Bodleian Library in 1973: Paul Morgan, *Oxford Libraries Outside the Bodleian*. This includes extensive information on unpublished materials in the libraries of colleges, faculties, departments and institutes. There is also a useful chapter on the University Archives. Less detailed information about unpublished sources in London libraries, collections can be found in *The Libraries of London*, edited by Raymond Irwin and Ronald Staveley (2nd ed., London, Library Association, 1961).

In an attempt to provide some assistance with searches for biographical information the Archives and Manuscripts Sub-committee of the Library Association's Research Committee in 1959 inaugurated a manuscripts survey. A wide variety of libraries, museums and record offices were circulated for information about their biographical materials. For obvious reasons the copyright libraries and the Public Record Office were excluded from the survey. Inevitably and reasonably the survey encountered difficulties and opposition from institutions because of lack of staff time to complete the questionnaire, or because the information was already recorded for the National Register of Archives. Nevertheless, entries for material relating to a total of 3,135 persons in 231 different repositories were collected and published as *Select Bio-graphical Sources: The Library Association Manuscripts Survey*, edited by Philip Hepworth (Library Association, 1971). The entries themselves are very brief. A typical entry is:

GROVE, *Sir* George (1820–1900).
    Writer on music.
    Letter   Bath P. L.
    Letters   Fitzwilliam Museum.

The greatest danger of the publication is, perhaps, that the student, not reading the introduction, will either assume that the work is more comprehensive than it claims to be, or will interpret the title as implying that the items have been carefully selected as representing the most important collections, rather than recognising that this is essentially a rather haphazard com-pilation in which selection is dependent upon the extent to which individual librarians and archivists were prepared to co-operate in completing the questionnaire. However, if the limitations of the work are recognised—and they are stated frankly in Mr. Hepworth's excellent introduction—*Select Biographical Sources* may well provide some useful guidance for the student. Certainly the introduction should be read, for it provides useful guidance on the search for biographical information. J. S. Batts, *British Manuscript Diaries of the Nine-teenth Century: an annotated listing* (Fontwell, Centaur Press,

1976) extends the coverage of this period by W. Matthews in his *British Diaries: an Annotated Bibliography* (Los Angeles, University of California, 1950).

Reports in Periodicals

Reports on collections of unpublished materials may appear irregularly in a wide variety of periodicals. Since it is clearly impossible for the student to check all possible periodicals, he must rely heavily on the existing subject indexes to current work. Information about these is given in Lionel Madden, *How To Find Out About the Victorian Period: A Guide to Sources of Information* (Oxford, Pergamon, 1970).

Regular descriptions of repositories or accumulations, notes on new deposits and other items of interest to the user as well as to the custodian of archives will be found in the principal professional and specialist periodicals relating to archives. The major British publications are twice-yearly journals: *Journal of the Society of Archivists* and British Records Association's periodical *Archives. Business Archives* is published by the Business Archives Council; the occasional *Newsletter* published by the Business Archives Council of Scotland is to be incorporated in *Scottish Industrial History* from 1976. The quarterly periodical, *The Local Historian*, formerly *The Amateur Historian* (National Council of Social Service), often includes useful articles on the location and nature of source materials.

The *British Studies Monitor* (Brunswick, Maine, Bowdoin College 1970–) includes regular information about work in progress and recently completed in the field of British studies by scholars in the United States, the United Kingdom and Commonwealth.

An interesting publication which may prove useful to students of the closing years of the 19th century is the periodical *Oral History: The Journal of the Oral History Society* (Department of Sociology, University of Essex, Wivenhoe Park, Colchester). The periodical includes articles by scholars using interviews, articles on sound archives and notes on current British work in oral history.

Publishing Projects

Recent years have seen a notable increase in the number of projects designed to publish comprehensive collections of the letters of 19th-century figures. More rigorous scholarly standards have revealed deficiences in the methods of earlier editors. The desire for greater accuracy, together with the discovery of unpublished letters, has led to the inauguration of many ambitious editorial projects. An illuminating account of the aims and methods of one such 19th-century project is given by Charles Richard Sanders in 'Editing the Carlyle letters: problems and opportunities', an essay in a collection entitled *Editing Nineteenth-Century Texts: Papers Given at the Editorial Conference, University of Toronto, November 1966,* edited by John M. Robson (Toronto, University Press, 1967). Another magnificent literary project is the Pilgrim Edition of *The Letters of Charles Dickens,* edited by Madeline House and Graham Storey (Oxford, Clarendon Press, 1965–). The editors estimate that the collection will include 'nearly 12,000 letters scattered over five continents'. This was joined in 1975 by the first volume (1843-75) of the *Letters of Henry James,* edited by Leon Edel (Macmillan). Obviously, the publication of correspondence is not confined to literary figures. Cambridge University Press recently issued *The Correspondence of Lord Overstone,* edited by D. P. O'Brien (3 vols., 1972).[2] Samuel Jones Loyd, Lord Overstone, was a banker and his letters written during 1804-83 are of considerable interest to the economic and political historian.

Information about recently published volumes of correspondence for many 19th-century persons can be conveniently traced in the annual 'Victorian Bibliography' which is published in the periodical *Victorian Studies* (Bloomington, Indiana University Press). The bibliography is arranged in four sections, the final section being devoted to an alphabetical sequence of individual authors. This includes a much wider range of persons than merely literary figures. Editions of an individual's correspondence are listed within this section along with editions of his writings and biographical and critical studies.

It is worth noting that few published editions of correspondence can hope to be absolutely definitive. Despite the best endeavours of editors, new material is always being discovered and a check in the indexes of the National

Register of Archives may well reveal newly-listed or obscurely-located manuscripts.

Two other large-scale publishing projects of source materials which are often difficult to locate may be mentioned here. *Sale Catalogues of Libraries of Eminent Persons,* under the general editorship of A. N. L. Munby (12 vols., Mansell, 1971–5) reprints photographically sale catalogues of figures notable in several important fields of activity. Volumes include sale catalogues of the libraries of literary figures, architects, politicians and scientists. The complete series of 10,000 catalogues of the sales held between 1733 and 1945 by Samuel Baker and his successors, now Sotheby & Co., has been reprinted in microfilm by University Microfilms Ltd. The catalogues are annotated with prices and buyers. An index of owners and a chronological list of all Sotheby sales has been compiled to accompany the microfilm. Inevitably, because of dispersal during his lifetime and the withholding of items from the sale by his family, sale catalogues do not always offer completely reliable guidance to an individual's library. Despite the necessity for caution in using them, however, they often constitute extremely valuable and elusive sources of information.

Substitute Sources

Details of 19th-century sources available in microform should be sought from the catalogues of the growing number of microform publishers.

Even if no original archive sources survive or can be traced, it can be gratifying to discover how much information can be traced from directories, year books and the local, trade or specialist press. To continue the search amongst original records it is necessary to have recourse to those classes of official records at local or national level in which the subject of research might be referred to and, more laboriously, to trace and check the archives of likely contacts and correspondents, whether individuals or institutions.

Exhibition catalogues may sometimes serve as a guide to obscure sources, including those in private hands. Archive facsimile sets, such as numerous repositories now issue for educational purposes, may be of use to those wishing to familiarise themselves with the original material before actually handling it. Checklists of such archive teaching units may be conveniently found in a series of articles by Robert G. E. Wood, entitled, 'Archive units for teaching history', in the issues of *Teaching History* for November 1971, May 1972, and May 1973. *The History Teachers' Yearbook* (Historical Association, 1976–) includes a list of archive teaching units.

When using 19th-century editions of correspondence due allowance should be made for differing editorial standards from those applied to modern editions of correspondence, and contemporary printed source material should be treated with appropriate reserve.

GUIDES TO COLLECTIONS OUTSIDE BRITAIN

BY FAR the most important guide to overseas manuscript sources for British studies is the American *National Union Catalog of Manuscript Collections.* The interest of North American collectors and institutions in British literary and historical manuscripts is no new phenomenon and the *National Union Catalog* is impressive not only in its scope but also in the richness of the accumulations which it covers. The first volume of the *Catalog,* covering returns made between 1959 and 1961, was published in 1962. From 1965 the series has been published by the Library of Congress in Washington. The returns in the first and all succeeding volumes list not only recent accessions, but all manuscripts acquired at any time prior to reporting and of any period. Within the compass of volumes containing entries for hundreds of accumulations each description is inevitably short. Despite this, it has proved possible to include lists of principal correspondents in many descriptions of *Nachlässe*. However, by no means every repository is covered by, nor every archive listed in, the *National Union Catalog.* Every research student is likely to have experience of a single unexpected document, identified in a detailed catalogue or discovered by chance when working through a collection of manuscripts, which is of prime importance for his own work, yet which falls through the wide mesh of the *National Union Catalog.*

Each volume of the *Catalog* explains the guiding principles of the editorial programme. Potential users of the *Catalog* will also find most helpful a comparative analysis of the *Catalog* and the National Register of Archives by Felicity Ranger in an article entitled 'The common pursuit'.[1] Information in the *Catalog* can be supplemented by a slightly older work, *A Guide to Archives and Manuscripts in the United States,* edited by Philip M. Hamer (New Haven, Yale University Press, 1961).

Since British and Commonwealth history are inextricably linked, at least for students of the 19th century, the existence of two union lists is important for researchers. The *Guide to Collections of Manuscripts Relating to Australia* first appeared in 1965 (Canberra, National Library of Australia). This is a loose-leaf, continuing publication, provided with binders and indexes, which gives a dozen or more lines of description of each accumulation, together with the usual details concerning covering dates, quantity, location and conditions of access. The *Union List of Manuscripts in Canadian Repositories* (Ottawa, Public Archives of Canada, 1968) is a single-volume guide to Canadian collections.

European lists, where they exist, fall somewhat outside the scope of the present work. As models of their kind, however, Wolfgang Mommsen, *Die Nachlässe in den deutschen Archiven (mit Ergänzungen aus anderen Beständen)* (Boppard, Harald Boldt Verlag, 1971) and its companion, *Nachlässe in den Bibliotheken der Bundesrepublik Deutschland,* compiled by Ludwig Denecke (Boppard, Harald Boldt Verlag, 1971) may be noted. The detail given in these, although much more restricted than in the Australian union list, for example, nevertheless enables a researcher to locate the *Nachlass* of a prominent German who might have corresponded with the British subject of his research.

SOME SPECIAL SUBJECT INTERESTS

MANY RESEARCH TOPICS do not fit neatly into a single convenient pigeon-hole. Even those to which a definite subject label can be attached will certainly involve the student in the examination of documents in a variety of fields of interest. In addition to checking systematically general sources of information and the catalogues of major archives, the student will need to discover what additional material may be located in specialised collections.

At first sight it might seem an impossible undertaking to attempt to present any kind of guide to the manifold subject fields in which researchers into the 19th century might be interested. It is indeed true that part of the expertise of the specialist lies in the knowledge which he has, often pains-takingly, acquired over the years of the sources relevant and available for his speciality. No single guide, directory or institution can hope, in the present state of affairs, to act as a substitute for this expertise. However, careful examination of the Historical Manuscripts Commission's *Record Repositories in Great Britain* (H.M.S.O.) will indicate major starting points for a variety of subject-orientated searches, even though the entries, with the exception of those for Greater London, are not arranged or indexed on a subject basis. What *Record Repositories* omits, as a matter of policy, are institutions, such as New College, London, or the Palestine Exploration Fund—to name but two at random—which hold records deriving from or relating to their main activity, but which are not primarily repositories, and are therefore not basically orientated to giving the kind of service the researcher has come to expect of a repository.

The viability of using *Record Repositories* as a starting point for a subject search might be tested by an examination of the sources for the study of 19th-century Congregationalism.

Record Repositories has references to the Congregational Library, Dr. Williams's Library, and the records of the London Missionary Society (which have recently been transferred to the care of the School of Oriental and African Studies of the University of London). Sources such as New College, London, cited above, are not indicated, although some at least of them—New College being a case in point—will be traceable through the National Register of Archives, as will also many of the deposits of the records of local congregations made in county and other record offices.

While the present work cannot provide any comprehensive survey of all possible fields of interest, the following paragraphs offer notes and references on guides to sources in a selection of the more important broad subject areas which will frequently be examined by students of the 19th century.

Architecture and the Visual Arts

Two repositories stand out with marked pre-eminence in this field: the Drawings Collection of the Royal Institute of British Architects (R.I.B.A.) and the Library and departmental collections of the Victoria and Albert Museum. The former, by its definition, concentrates on architecture, although there is material relating to furniture design in the case of such architects as A. W. N. Pugin, whose designing activity extended to interiors and furnishings. In 1972 the Drawings Collection moved to a separate building (21 Portman Square, London, W.1), and the bulk of the R.I.B.A.'s manuscript holdings were transferred with the drawings to this address. The first volume of *A Catalogue of Architectural Drawings in the Drawings Collection of the Royal Institute of British Architects* was published in 1969 (Farnborough, Gregg). Many of the deposited manuscripts, in some cases closely related to the drawings, have been listed by the staff of the Historical Manuscripts Commission, and copies of completed lists are available at the National Register of Archives, the R.I.B.A., and the national libraries. Some manuscripts remain in the library, including prize essays and manuscripts grangerised in the bound Pamphlets and Early Works series. All requests to consult manuscripts, whether in the Drawings Collection or in the Library, should be addressed to the Librarian at 66 Portland Place, London, W1N 4AD.

The holdings of the Victoria & Albert Museum include large and important deposits of architectural plans, such as those of E. W. Godwin, but they also extend over the whole range of arts and crafts, including furniture, pottery, jewellery, textile and theatre design, as well as the literary manuscripts referred to elsewhere and theatre material outside the field of stage design.[1] An excellent concise (but unindexed) descriptive guide to some of the departmental material was published in 1964: *Handbook to the Departments of Prints and Drawings and Paintings* (H.M.S.O.).

National sources are, of course, by no means limited to these two repositories. The extensive autograph collections of the Fitzwilliam Museum in Cambridge include a considerabe quantity of 19th-century artists' letters. The as yet partially-catalogued holdings of the Royal Academy of Arts, on which the staff of the Historical Manuscripts Commission is currently working, promise to provide sources for 19th-century painting. There are also specialised repositories such as the William Morris Gallery (Water House, Lloyd Park, Forest Road, Walthamstow, London E17 4PP)[2] maintained by the London Borough of Waltham Forest, which also includes papers of Mackmurdo; the Ruskin Gallery, Bembridge, Isle of Wight; and the De Wint Centre, Usher Art Gallery, Lincoln, the establishment of which was announced in November 1972. Local record offices hold much architectural material, representing the work of national as well as local architects, in estate and parish records, and such deposits as those of the Board of Education school plans and the Church Commissioners parsonage house papers.

The records of local authorities generally may be of value, either in their role as clients or as planning controllers. Urban development and town planning will, at least to some extent, be illuminated by the records of solicitors, estate agents and land-owners and, increasingly, by the deposit of deeds for sites sometimes extending over a large area, which have been re-developed in the second half of the 20th century. In 1966 Westminster City Archives achieved national status in the field of furniture history by their purchase of the Waring & Gillow archive.

The publication of *Architectural History and the Fine and Applied Arts: Sources in the National Register of Archives* is referred to in Chapter 2 above. Although this covers all periods it lists a considerable amount of 19th-century material. William E. Fredeman, *Pre-Raphaelitism: A Bibliocritical Study* (Cambridge, Harvard University Press, 1965) includes extensive information about the location and contents of archive collections in this field.

For a guide to architectural drawings in American collections reference should be made to John Harris, *Catalogue of British Drawings for Architecture, Decoration, Sculpture and Landscape Gardening, 1550–1900, in American Collections* (Upper Saddle River, N.J., Gregg Press, 1971).

It is sadly true that for the student of architecture the physical evidence of the buildings themselves and their layout is a source which diminishes in extent with each week that passes, forcing the researcher back to the written, printed and graphic evidence, unsupported by the three-dimensional actuality.[3] Surviving buildings as diverse as churches and terrace cottages may bear external evidence as to their original owners, architects or builders, and the date of construction or restoration in the form of foundation stones, date or name plaques of stone or other materials, dates, etc., incorporated in the actual brickwork, using multi-coloured bricks, or even on cast-iron tie-plates or rainwater heads.[4]

For a *verbal* topographical description of early Victorian England (the bare bones of which can be clothed by prints and later by photographs), the various editions of Samuel Lewis, *A Topographical Dictionary of England* of the 1830s and 1840s are invaluable. The locality descriptions in *Kelly's Directories*, fulfil this function in the latter part of the century, especially in relation to public buildings. An excellent introduction to the main published cartographic sources is *The Historian's Guide to Ordnance Survey Maps*, by J. B. Harley (Standing Conference for Local History, 1964).

Business History

Business history is likely to be involved in almost every aspect of 19th-century studies at some time or other. The

19th-century witnessed a number of important organisational developments in the business sphere, not least of which was the inception of the limited liability company in 1855. (The records of dissolved companies in the Public Record Office [BT.31] are a useful source.)

It is impossible to generalise about surviving 19th-century business records. Much has been destroyed; much remaining in the custody of firms is inaccessible; some has been deposited, mostly, it is probably true to say, of smaller businesses, though this is not to deny their cumulative importance in the economy and their individual significance at local level. There has been a welcome tendency in the post-war period for firms to appoint archivists and some are listed in *Record Repositories in Great Britain* (H.M.S.O.). However, it should not be assumed that the existence of an archivist necessarily means that records are available to outside researchers. It is difficult to generalise about how to approach firms which have no archivist: the public relations department is an obvious starting point, but there may be no direct access from there to records in the custody of administrative or financial departments.

Only one body in England and Wales is solely concerned with business records. The Business Archives Council was founded in 1934 with the aims of encouraging the preservation of business records and the writing of business history. Its original intention of compiling a national register of business records has largely been superseded by the accumulation of information on business archives in the National Register of Archives. (The publication by the Historical Manuscripts Commission of *Sources of Business History in the National Register of Archives* has been noted in Chapter 2.) Three main aspects of the Business Archives Council's current work are of special interest to those pursuing 19th-century studies. These are its library, its policy of conducting surveys of the records of certain spheres of business activity, and its journal.

The library, which is maintained at the Council's offices, comprises an important collection of business histories, mostly published since 1945, many of which deal at length with the 19th century. A duplicated guide to the first acquisitions—*The First Five Hundred*—was produced in 1959 and is still available from the Council (price 25p post free). The first published survey, of the records of the shipping industry, *Shipping: A Survey of Historical Records,* edited by P. Mathias and A. W. H. Pearsall, was published in 1971 (Newton Abbot, David & Charles). This survey was undertaken by the Business Archives Council in conjunction with the National Maritime Museum. Much work has already been done on a thorough survey of the records of banking under the direction of Professor L. S. Pressnell, the results of which are intended for eventual publication. A survey of insurance records begun in 1972 has produced *The British Insurance Business, 1547-1970* by H. A. L. Cockerell & E. Green (Heinemann, 1976).[5]

As its journal the Council publishes *Business Archives* twice yearly in June and December. (Since 1974 financial problems have interfered with this schedule.) This is issued free to individual and institutional members. *Business Archives* contains major articles on different aspects of business records, shorter descriptions of particular archives, notes and news, reviews and notices of recently-published business histories, and other relevant works, and a bibliography, as well as an annual abstract of deposited business records, based on the Historical Manuscripts Commission's *Accessions to Repositories.* The Council also issues *Newsletters* and *Broadsheet* series.

All enquiries about the Business Archives Council should be addressed to the Secretary, Business Archives Council, Dominion House, 37–45 Tooley Street, London Bridge, London, S.E.1.

A similar, though younger, council exists in Scotland. This has already sponsored the listing of some important Scottish business archives. Its occasional duplicated *Newsletter*, edited by Professor P. L. Payne, of Aberdeen University, included short articles on its work and on Scottish business records. All enquiries about the Scottish Business Archives Council should be addressed to its Secretary, W. Lind, 'Throsk', Kilbarchan Road, Bridge of Weir, Renfrewshire.[6]

Further information about the sources of business history may be derived from the useful introductory pamphlet by T. C. Barker, R. H. Campbell and P. Mathias, *Business History* (rev. ed., Historical Association, 1971), and from *Management and Control of Business Records* (Business Archives Council, 1966. Revised edition in preparation), and *London Business House Histories: A Handlist* (Guildhall Library, 1964). For inventors in the first half of the 19th century see Bennet Woodcroft, *Alphabetical Index of Patentees of Inventions, 1617–1852* (1854, reprinted with revisions, Evelyn, Adams & Mackay, 1969). Two year-books which are generally useful are *The Stock Exchange Official Year-Book* (Croydon, Skinner), and the *Register of Defunct and Other Companies Removed from the Stock Exchange Official Year-Book* (Croydon, Skinner).

In conclusion, at least passing reference must be made to the records of agricultural activity. Farm records, principally accounts, are to be found in varying quantities in most county record offices, many are recorded in the Subject Index of the National Register of Archives, and Reading University Library has many copies or originals, as a result of surveys carried out by the Institute of Agricultural History, Reading University.[7] Records of landed estates, estate agents, valuers and auctioneers and of agriculture-based or related crafts and occupations or material related to them, such as deeds, are also to be found in some quantity in county and other local record offices, and will supplement farm records in illustrating the state of agriculture in a particular area.[8] A survey of the records of the agricultural engineering industry has recently been undertaken by the Institute of Agricultural History.

Education

A helpful introduction to the complex field of educational provision and the correspondingly complex records situation will be found in Chapter 10 of Alan Rogers, *This Was Their World: Approaches to Local History* (B.B.C., 1972). This draws attention to national as well as the more obvious local records, those of central government and of the two great 19th-century societies, the British and Foreign Schools Society and the National Society. (The latter features in *Record Repositories in Great Britain* [H.M.S.O.], but the former apparently lost the bulk of its records in the Second World War.) On a local level, education records should be sought primarily in the record office of those local authorities which are, or have been, education authorities, the counties and county boroughs.[9] Parish records, which may be deposited, may contain National School records. School plans for the Board of Education have been mentioned elsewhere. Malcolm Seaborne, *The English School: Its Architecture and Organization, 1370–1870* (Routledge, 1971) provides a well-documented and illustrated introduction to buildings of the period before Forster's Education Act.

Apart from the public schools—Eton, for example, has an archivist—records of the private sector (fee-paying education) for the 19th century are likely to be sparse, many smaller establishments probably being represented by a stray letter, account, or circular or advertisement in a local newspaper. On the other hand, the archives of many middle and upper class families will include correspondence with or about sons at public schools and possibly about the tuition of daughters.

The records of special purpose educational institutions should not be overlooked, such as those of New College, London, or St. Edmund's College, near Ware, which are mentioned in another context. An outstanding individual archive promises to be revealed when the 40,000 or so in-letters of Oscar Browning (1837–1923) from Hastings Public Library have been sorted and a summary list prepared by the staff of the Historical Manuscripts Commission. A historian and educationalist, Oscar Browning, of Eton and King's College, Cambridge, was Principal of the Cambridge University Day Training College and had a wide-ranging correspondence with schoolteachers, including his own students who went into the profession, as well as with eminent historians and other academics.

In the field of higher education the existence of such university archives as those of Cambridge[10] and Liverpool, which hold records of their respective universities as distinct from or as well as deposits of other records, should be noted. The published *Letters of Frederic William Maitland* (Downing Professor of the Laws of England from 1888)[11] may be mentioned in this context, as they are by no means restricted in interest to legal history and give a vivid picture of the

late 19th-century scholarly world. The possibility of such
records of education as school or university notebooks
from the late Victorian period surviving among recently-
deposited *Nachlässe* should not be overlooked, although they
may be untypical in that they derive from particularly gifted
individuals.[12]

Imperialism

As a main theme of 19th-century history the sources for the
study of imperialism are inextricably linked with the papers
of politicians and military leaders, as well as with business
records such as those of Jardine Matheson & Co., the Far East
merchants, in Cambridge University Library, and with the
various missionary societies.[13] Imperialism will also feature
in the papers of 19th-century writers and commentators on
public affairs. Thus, for example, surviving letters to T. H. S.
Escott, editor of the *Fortnightly Review,* which have recently
been listed by the Historical Manuscripts Commission, reflect
the interest in imperial policy shown in the columns of the
Fortnightly.

The following are some of the principal repositories in this
field: the Public Record Office;[14] the India Office Library
and Records;[15] the National Army Museum; the National
Maritime Museum; Rhodes House Library and St. Antony's
College, Oxford; the Sudan Centre, Durham University; the
School of Oriental and African Studies Library, London
University; and the Royal Commonwealth Society Library,
London.[16] An important series of regional guides to manuscript material in the British Isles relating to the areas of
colonial activity is being prepared through the agency of the
School of Oriental and African Studies. Published volumes
include *A Guide to Western Manuscripts and Documents
in the British Isles Relating to South and South-East Asia*
(O.U.P., 1965), and *A Guide to Manuscripts and Documents
in the British Isles Relating to Africa* (O.U.P., 1971). A guide
to the manuscript sources for the history of Australia, New
Zealand and the Pacific Islands, edited with Australian sponsor-
ship by Miss P. Mander-Jones, was published in late 1972
(Canberra, Australian National University Press).

Literature

There is an almost overwhelming diversity of possible sources for literary studies. In general, however, there are three broad categories of repository in which manuscripts of literary works and unpublished materials relating to literary figures are most likely to be located:

1. The national libraries. For these the student is referred to the guides and catalogues listed in Chapter 3.

2. Single-author accumulations, perhaps based on a major archive group as a nucleus, with collected material added. These are often found in local libraries in areas specially associated with the writer. Examples of such collections are the Dickens manuscripts in Dickens House (48 Doughty Street, London, W.C.1); the Hardy manuscripts in Dorset County Museum (High West Street, Dorchester, Dorset); and the holdings of the Tennyson Research Centre in Lincoln City Library (Free School Lane, Lincoln).[16a] Such collections can often be traced in the *Aslib Directory* and other works noted in Chapter 5 and may be available in microform.

3. Manuscripts purchased by American university and other libraries. Some of these may be located by use of the *National Union Catalog of Manuscript Collections* and *A Guide to Archives and Manuscripts in the United States,* edited by Philip M. Hamer, both discussed in Chapter 6.

In addition, there are, inevitably, sources which do not fit into any of the above categories. One example is the Forster Bequest of Dickens and other literary material in the Victoria & Albert Museum Library.[17] Moreover, it is important to remember that literary figures will usually have many friendships and social contacts extending outside the literary world. In the papers of Field Marshal Lord Wolseley, for example, in Hove Central Library, we find letters from Ouida, Vernon Lee, Andrew Lang, and Henry James, as well as from the more predictable military figures.

A further fruitful source of information may be the archives of the author's publishers, if these survive. For some information about this see the section on publishing below.

Military and Naval History

The principal national repositories, apart from the Public Record Office where the Admiralty and War Office classes are particularly relevant, are the National Army Museum, Chelsea (formerly at Camberley, and including the Indian Army in its scope)[18] and the National Maritime Museum, Greenwich.[19] In addition, there are numerous regimental and corps museums throughout the country, many of which hold manuscripts. A useful checklist is provided by N. Wise, *A Guide to Military Museums* (Bracknell, Bellona Publications, no date). Private papers, deposited and undeposited, include military and naval material from all ranks of the services, one of the most notable local deposits being the papers of Field Marshal Viscount Wolseley in Hove Central Library. These have been enriched in recent years by the transfer of the Wolseley deposit formerly in the Royal United Services Institute. (At the same time the Institute transferred all its other manuscript holdings, principally to the National Army Museum.) Records of local volunteer forces, militia and yeomanry, will be found in the Public Record Office and in local repositories. J. D. Sainsbury, *Hertfordshire's Soldiers: A Survey of the Auxiliary Military Forces Raised in Hertfordshire from 1757 to the Present Day* (Hitchin, Hertfordshire Local History Council, 1969), although dealing basically with one county, gives a good idea of the spread of the sources.

A Guide to the Sources of British Military History, edited by Robin Higham (Routledge, 1972) devotes considerable space to the military history of the 19th and 20th centuries. The work gives much useful advice on how to obtain access to special collections and private archives.

Politics

The broad outlines of a guide to sources for political history at a national level can be drawn with reference above all to the principal archives of its main protagonists. Notable examples of such archives are: the Disraeli Papers at Hughenden; the Palmerston Papers owned by the Broadlands Trust, and on long temporary deposit with the Historical Manuscripts Commission,[20] and his letter books in the British

Library; the Gladstone Papers in the British Library,[21] at Hawarden,[22] and in Lambeth Palace Library;[23] the papers of the third Marquess of Salisbury on long-term deposit at Christ Church, Oxford; and the Joseph Chamberlain Papers in Birmingham University Library. Such *Nachlässe* complement the holdings of the Public Record Office; it should, of course, be remembered that the private papers of those who held office in the 19th century are likely to include material which would today find its way into official custody.

Through the work of the Twentieth Century Political Records Survey, financed by the Social Science Research Council and based on the British Library of Political and Economic Science, information is now available on the holdings of the two party organisations—the Liberal Central Association minutes and deposits at the National Liberal Club, and the holdings of the Conservative Party machine, including the Conservative Central Office. The Labour Party archives are outside the scope of this *Guide,* the Labour Representation Committee having been founded in 1900, but it should be noted that the Labour Party archives include small deposits relating to Bronterre O'Brien, Henry Vincent and H. A. Barker and the Labour Union, all of which have been listed by the Historical Manuscripts Commission. The *Dictionary of Labour Biography,* edited by Joyce M. Bellamy and John Saville (Macmillan, 1972–   ) has become an important biographical source for 19th-century political researchers, its value being enhanced by the details of manuscript sources which are a feature of some of the biographies. The records of the Independent Labour Party, formed in 1893, have been catalogued with the support of a grant from the Social Science Research Council. Records of the Fabian Society (1884) are housed in Nuffield College, Oxford.

The detail of the picture is provided by the records of non-Cabinet politicians, including radicals, Chartists and those involved in the labour and trade union movements,[24] the records of national and local political associations and pressure groups and of political writers, commentators and editors.

Not all of these categories of records are easily to be found and some will have to be sought overseas, for example in the holdings of the International Institute of Social History,

Amsterdam. John R. Vincent's introduction and list of manuscript sources in *The Formation of the British Liberal Party 1857-1868* (Constable, 1966, reprinted Penguin, 1972) give a brief but very clear introduction to the kind of sources which are sought and which may survive for the study of 19th-century political history: the papers of Cabinet politicians, of radical parliamentarians (and those of other political leanings, depending on one's field of research), and the records of local party organisations and of militant national societies. Non-manuscript sources will include local news-papers and ephemera such as pollbooks in local history collections.[25]

It is possibly only on a local level that real 'discoveries' of sources are still to be made.[26] On a national level the researcher should keep in touch with the work in progress on the 19th-century *Prime Ministers' Papers* project, which is discussed in Chapter 2. The Political Records Survey's first volume, *Sources in British Political History 1900-1951: The Archives of Selected Organisations & Societies* (Macmillan, 1975) gives details of re-cords of numerous bodies founded pre-1900.

Postal History

The study of postal history is not an essential preparation for the researcher, but an awareness of the evidential value of postmarks, especially as an aid to the dating of correspondence, is recommended. Attention to postal markings can be par-ticularly helpful when overseas correspondence is being dealt with, enabling the travelling time of letters and the time lag in an exchange of correspondence to be ascertained. For inland correspondence familiarity with the usual abbreviations of the months (MR, MY, JU, JY, etc.) employed in date-stamps and the actual make-up of the postmarks can help to determine the dates of letters, as can attention paid to the practice of postmarking letters by the post office of receipt as well as despatch ('arrival marks'). It is vital for those working on uncatalogued records to preserve the relationship of letters and envelopes, as this may be the only sure way of dating the correspondence.

The establishment of the *Uniform Penny Post* (*local* penny posts had existed previously) and the introduction of the adhesive postage stamp in 1840 and subsequent postal developments, such as the setting up of the Universal Postal Union,[27] in themselves together constitute one of the major achievements of the 19th century, with an impact on communications so great that it is paradoxically easy to overlook it or take it for granted. One such development is described by Anthony Trollope in Chapter 5 of his *Autobiography*:

> Early in 1851 I was upon a special job of official work, which for two years so completely absorbed my time that I was able to write nothing. A plan was formed for extending the rural delivery of letters, and for adjusting the work, which up to that time had been done in a very irregular manner . . . The object was to create a postal network which should catch all recipients of letters . . . In all these visits I was, in truth, a beneficent angel to the public, bringing everywhere with me an earlier, cheaper, and much more regular delivery of letters.

The Rev. Dr. John Pye Smith of Homerton College, writing after the introduction of uniform penny postage, but before the introduction of the adhesive postage stamp, commented to his son that no small increase of work accrued from the Post Office reform, '. . . yet it is a glorious blessing "for a' that" '.[28]

The innovations of 1840 led to the growth of the postal system, which was of course linked to the communications revolution associated with the development of the railway system,[29] and had important repercussions in the fields of design and printing,[30] and on the economy, for example in relation to labour, transport and *matériel*. The basic historical records for the study of this phenomenon will be found in the Post Office Archives, but there is important additional source material in the Reginald E. Phillips' Collection of Nineteenth-Century Stamps in the National Postal Museum (King Edward Building, King Edward Street, London, E.C.1). An excellent *Short Account* of the collection by F. Marcus Arman (1966) is available from the museum. Two major published works will serve as a guide to British postage stamps from 1840 onwards and as an introduction to the subject of postmarks: Robson Lowe, *The British Postage Stamp of the Nineteenth Century* (National Postal Museum, 1968), and R. C. Alcock and F. C. Holland, *British Postmarks: A Short History and Guide* (2nd ed., Cheltenham, R. C. Alcock, 1970).

The numbered stamps allocated to post offices in 1844 are identified in G. Brumell, *British Post Office Numbers, 1844–1906* (rev. ed., Cheltenham, R. C. Alcock, 1972). For a guide to the literature see Arnold M. Strange, *A List of Books on the Postal History, Postmarks and Adhesive Postage and Revenue Stamps of Great Britain* (2nd ed., Brighton, G. B. Philatelic Society, 1971). Much evidence on local postal services will, of course, be found in deposits of all kinds in local record offices, although a good deal of 'collectable' material is in the hands of private postal history collectors, and therefore not always readily accessible.

It is appropriate to mention in this section a late-19th-century development of great potential significance for communications and records, namely the invention of the telephone by Alexander Graham Bell, and its commercial establishment as a communications network. The system in the United Kingdom was not initially a monopoly of the G.P.O.; the first commercial telephone company was registered in June 1878 and a mixed system of commercial companies and the Post Office, as well as a few local authorities, provided telephonic communications until the G.P.O. monopoly came into operation at the beginning of 1912. The impact of the use of the telephone on conventional record-keeping can only be surmised;[31] for our period it is probably true to say that it was relatively slight. For a history of the telecommunications industry in Britain, see J. H. Robertson, *The Story of the Telephone* (Pitman, 1947). The reprint of *Three Victorian Telephone Directories* of 1884–5 (Newton Abbot, David and Charles, 1970) provides an opportunity to examine lists of early subscribers. For an account of the earlier phenomenon of the technical and commercial development of the electric telegraph and some consideration of its role in communications and social and economic life, J. L. Kieve, *The Electric Telegraph: A Social and Economic History* (Newton Abbot, David and Charles, 1973) should be consulted.

Publishing

Inevitably, the records of many 19th-century publishers have perished either because of the death of the firm or because of misfortune. The majority of the archives of Cassell & Co. Ltd., for example, were destroyed in an air raid in 1941. Thus, in writing *The House of Cassell 1848-1958* (Cassell, 1958), Simon Nowell-Smith had to rely largely on published reminiscences and the recollections of members of the staff. Where records have survived they are frequently held by the publisher or his successors. Thus many records of the correspondence and accounts of George Allen, Ruskin's publisher, are still in the care of Allen & Unwin.[32]

Some records, of course, have found their way into public collections. The correspondence files of Richard Bentley & Son were purchased by the University of Illinois, though some letters are also in the Bodleian Library and the Berg Collection of the New York Public Library. The surviving business records of Bentley are in the British Library. These manuscripts have been studied by Royal A. Gettmann, in *A Victorian Publisher: A Study of the Bentley Papers* (C.U.P., 1960). The papers of the Edinburgh publishing house of William Blackwood & Sons (to 1900) are in the National Library of Scotland.[33] These consist mainly of letters written by authors to Blackwood, but also include some manuscripts and proofs of works considered for publication. This collection of the firm's incoming material is listed in the third volume of the National Library of Scotland's *Catalogue of Manuscripts* under the title *Blackwood Papers 1805-1900* (Edinburgh, H.M.S.O., 1968). The letter-books, which contain copies of outgoing correspondence, have remained in the possession of the firm. The main sequence of Macmillan papers is housed in the British Library, although a valuable collection of miscellaneous correspondence is in the University of Reading Library. A selection of *Letters to Macmillan,* edited by Simon Nowell-Smith, was published by Macmillan in 1967.[34]

The University of Reading is currently attempting to build up an archive of British publishing by inviting publishers to deposit their older records in the University Library. The library aims to produce a catalogue of each deposit. Only records of more than 30 years old will be available for consultation by the public and depositing publishers may also impose other conditions if they wish.

Archives of certain British publishers are being made available on microfilm by Chadwyck-Healey Ltd. (54 South Street, Bishops Stortford, Herts.). The first group of microfilms, issued during 1974, include the archives of George Allen & Co., 1893–1915; Cambridge University Press, 1696–1902; Elkin Mathews, 1811–1938; Kegan Paul, Trench, Trübner & Henry S. King, 1858–1912; George Routledge & Co., 1853–1902; and Swan Sonnenschein & Co., 1878–1911. A printed *Guide to the Archives of the Cambridge University Press*, by E. S. Leedham-Green has been published and new printed indexes have been compiled for each archive except Mathews and Routledge. A catalogue of the Elkin Mathews collection and indexes of the Routledge collection are included on the relevant microfilms.

Information about 19th-century periodicals and newspapers is elusive. The records of major publishers will, of course, reveal information about their activities in this field. Many useful studies of specific titles are listed by Sheila and Henry Rosenberg in the *New Cambridge Bibliography of English Literature, Vol. III: 1800–1900* (C.U.P., 1969). *The Nineteenth-Century Periodical Press in Britain: A Bibliography of Modern Studies, 1901–1971*, compiled by Lionel Madden and Diana Dixon (Toronto, Victorian Periodicals Newsletter, 1975) is an extensive listing of published and unpublished studies. *The British Union-Catalogue of Periodicals* (Butterworths) and the *Union List of Serials in Libraries of the United States and Canada* (New York, H. W. Wilson) record library holdings of periodicals. The first phase of a directory of Victorian periodicals has recently been published by the University of Waterloo.[35] Details of this and other work in progress on the history of 19th-century periodicals and newspapers, together with notes of new discoveries, may be conveniently found in the *Victorian Periodicals Newsletter* (1968–   ), issued by the Research Society for Victorian Periodicals. One of the Society's current projects is a survey of manuscript sources that are relevant to the study of Victorian periodicals.

The papers of prominent individuals may, of course, include correspondence with editors about the preparation and publication of articles. The recent listing of some of the in-letters of one of these editors, T. H. S. Escott, of the *Fortnightly Review,* by the Royal Commission on Historical Manuscripts may be noted in this context.

Behind publishing lies the printing industry. In this field the Printing Historical Society and its *Journal* (The Society, 1965–) and the holdings of the St. Bride Library (St. Bride's Institute, Bride Lane, Fleet Street, London, E.C.4.) are especially important, in addition to sources noted in the section on Printed Ephemera in Chapter 8.

Religious History

Some indication of essential sources has already been given in the introduction to this chapter. For the Established Church the basic pattern is provided by the designation of certain county record offices as Diocesan Record Offices, by Diocesan Registries and Cathedral libraries, and by the surveys of parish records which have been undertaken by many county record offices, resulting in numerous cases in the deposit of records. Typescript copies of the findings of a *Survey of Ecclesiastical Archives* carried out under the auspices of the Pilgrim Trust in 1952 are deposited in the British Library, Lambeth Palace Library, the Bodleian Library and Cambridge University Library. Dorothy M. Owen, *The Records of the Established Church in England Excluding Parochial Records* (British Records Association, 1970) is an admirable scholarly survey of a complex record field. Lambeth Palace Library has published a number of catalogues. E. G. W. Bill's *Catalogue of Manuscripts in Lambeth Palace Library: MSS. 1222-1860* (Oxford, Clarendon Press, 1972), which continues from Todd's catalogue of 1812, covers a surprising diversity of 19th-century sources. Amongst individual catalogues, the *Catalogue of the Papers of Roundell Palmer (1812-1895), First Earl of Selborne,* the high churchman, also compiled by E. G. W. Bill (Lambeth Palace Library, 1967) may be cited as of particular interest to 19th-century researchers. For York diocesan records, David M. Smith, *Guide to the Archive Collections in the Borthwick*

Institute of Historical Research (University of York, 1973) is an indispensable introduction (supplements in B.I. *Bulletin*).

At a local level, the surveying and acceptance of deposits has extended mainly to the Protestant denominations. Many sources of information are listed in *Archives of Religious and Ecclesiastical Bodies and Organisations Other than the Church of England* (British Records Association, 1936). More up-to-date information about the records of specific denominations may be traced in the periodicals of their historical societies, such as *Proceedings of the Wesley Historical Society* and *Journal of the Friends' Historical Society*. The general archivists' periodicals noted in Chapter 5 will also prove helpful. In 1964, for example, *Archives* included a survey of 'Archives and manuscripts in nonconformist libraries', by C. E. Welch.[36]

Far fewer Roman Catholic church records have been surveyed or deposited in county record offices, Lancashire being a major exception, at least in so far as returns to the National Register of Archives are concerned. However, repositories have been established, for example in seminaries, in a number of dioceses. The seminaries themselves in some instances have extensive manuscript holdings: amongst recent additions to the National Register of Archives is a 515pp. list of the archives of St. Edmund's College, Old Hall Green, near Ware, Hertfordshire, compiled by J. Kitching of the Institute of Education, Durham University (N.R.A. 16303). One major published source of 19th-century religious history which must be mentioned is the monumental edition of *The Letters and Diaries of John Henry Newman,* edited by C. S. Dessain (Nelson, 1961–　).

A useful brief introduction to, and bibliography of, Christian socialism is provided by Stanley Evans, *Christian Socialism: A Study Outline and Bibliography* (Christian Socialist Movement, 1962). For the records of missionary activity of the churches overseas a most helpful starting point is provided by Rosemary Keen, *Survey of the Archives of Selected Missionary Societies* (typescript, reproduced by Historical Manuscripts Commission, 1968, and still available).

It is perhaps worth emphasising that many classes of ecclesiastical archives contain information of general and social historical interest (such as emigration material in Anglican parish records), as well as sources for architectural history in fabric records.

Science and Technology

The results of a wide-ranging survey by a group at Sussex University under the direction of Dr. Roy MacLeod into the surviving papers, deposited or in private hands, of scientists at all levels who were active between 1850 and 1914 have been published in microfiche with an accompanying index and guide under the title *Archives of British Men of Science* (Mansell, 1972). It is likely, however, that further sources illustrating the role of scientists in industry remain in the (often uncatalogued) archives of business firms. Publication of a *Guide* to the manuscripts of scientists from the 17th century to the time of Rutherford, which is being prepared by Maddison & Craig for the Standing Joint Committee of the Royal Society and the Historical Manuscripts Commission, is forecast, but rather overdue.[37]

For science as for other subjects some published sources are available, such as *Selected Correspondence of Michael Faraday*, edited by L. Pearce Williams (2 vols., C.U.P., 1971), and *Darwin and Henslow, the Growth of an Idea: Letters 1831–1860,* edited by Nora Barlow (Murray, 1967). As an example of a printed descriptive list, in this case of variously located material, there is the monumental *Banks Letters*, edited by Warren R. Dawson (British Museum [Natural History], 1958, with *Supplementary Letters,* 1962, 1965), listing the correspondence of Sir Joseph Banks, who, although perhaps remembered primarily as an 18th-century figure, remained active until his death in 1820.

If any single location of scientific manuscripts is to be mentioned it should be the South Kensington area of London (S.W.7), where are situated the holdings of the Science Museum, which include papers of Charles Babbage, as well as deposits relating primarily to applied science (unfortunately no overall catalogue is available); the archives of Imperial College of Science and Technology, which include the Thomas Huxley Papers, listed by Warren R. Dawson in a *Catalogue* (Macmillan, 1946); the varied holdings of the British Museum (Natural History), recently described in *A Short History of the Libraries and List of Manuscripts and Original Drawings in the British Museum (Natural History)* (British Museum [Natural History], 1971);[38] and the Institute of Geological Sciences, incorporating the Geological Survey and the Museum of Practical Geology.

Another concentration of 19th-century scientific manuscripts will be found in Cambridge, including the papers of William Whewell in Trinity College, the Darwin Manuscripts in the University Library, and the holdings of the Scott Polar Research Institute, which include manuscripts on polar exploration, flora and fauna, and oceanography. Another potential source is the holdings of the libraries and archives of learned societies and institutions in London and other major cities, which is still something of an uncharted area. Thus the Royal Aeronautical Society in London includes such pre-Wright brothers material as the papers of Sir George Cayley (on loan) and the engine drawings of the Australian aviation pioneer, Lawrence Hargrave.

The greatest British collection of source materials for the history of medicine is found in the Library of the Wellcome Institute of the History of Medicine (183 Euston Road, London, N.W.1). The Institute publishes the quarterly periodicals *Medical History* and *Current Work in the History of Medicine*. The Library's holdings include western and oriental manuscripts and a large number of autograph letters on all aspects of medical history. Nineteenth-century manuscripts in the Library are listed in S. A. J. Moorat, *Catalogue of Western Manuscripts on Medicine and Science in the Wellcome Historical Medical Library* (2 vols. in 3, London, Wellcome Institute, 1962–73).

Guidance on other collections of manuscript material, such as the important holdings of correspondence in the libraries of the Royal Colleges, is given in the first chapter of John L. Thornton, *Medical Librarianship: Principles and Practice* (Crosby Lockwood, 1963), in the second volume of the *Aslib Directory* (Aslib, 1970: see Chapter 5 above), and in *Directory of Medical Libraries in the British Isles* (3rd ed., Library Association, 1969).

Transport

The 19th century witnessed a transport revolution based on the employment of the steam engine as a prime mover, giving rise to the railway system, the steam ship and, later, the agricultural and general purpose traction engine. For railways, the principal archive source is the British Transport Historical Records, for which the Public Record Office assumed responsibility on 1 April 1972. The records at Porchester Road are to be transferred to the new Public Record Office building at Kew when it is completed. The British Transport Historical Records also include the records of canal companies which had been absorbed by the railway undertakings.

Other significant sources for the study of railways are listed in George Ottley, *Railway History: A Guide to Sixty-One Collections in Libraries and Archives in Great Britain* (Library Association, Reference, Special and Information Section, 1973). Entries are based on answers to a questionnaire. Each entry includes a useful evaluation of the scope and significance of the collections listed. To the detailed list of collections is added a succinct note on 'Railway history in local record offices'. This may be supplemented by an article by Jack Simmons in the *Journal of Transport History* on 'Railway history in English local records',[39] C. R. Clinker's pamphlet, *Railway History: A Handlist of the Principal Sources of Original Material with Notes and Guidance on its Use* (The Author, Trvorwyn, Harlyn Bay, Cornwall), and E. H. Fowkes, *Railway History and the Local Historian* (York, East Yorkshire Local History Society, 1963). George Ottley, *A Bibliography of British Railway History* (Allen & Unwin, 1965), of course, includes an enormous amount of useful information, and there is a regular supply of information in the *Journal of Transport History* (Leicester, University Press, 1953–   ).

The development of another form of railed transport, street tramways, was a feature of the second half of the 19th century, successively horse-, steam-, and electric-powered. The records of the municipal successors to the original private companies may be sought in the appropriate local record offices.

As far as shipping is concerned, *Shipping: A Survey of Historical Records,* edited by P. Mathias and A. W. H. Pearsall (Newton Abbot, David & Charles, 1971) is probably the best starting point, although there are some notable omissions. The National Maritime Museum is the principal repository for civil marine as well as naval archives, supplemented by the local repositories of the major port towns (note also the records of the Cunard Steam-Ship Co. Ltd. in Liverpool University Archives). This local shipping material was added to in many repositories in 1971 by the transfer from the Public Record Office of crew lists, log books and agreements of merchant and fishing vessels from the 1860s to the eve of the First World War, being part of the former records of the Registrar of Shipping and Seamen and material deposited under the Merchant Shipping (Fishing Boats) Act, 1883. The principal journal is *The Mariner's Mirror* (Society for Nautical Research, 1911-   ).

The same scarcity factors seem to apply to shipbuilding and locomotive constructors' records, as operate in the field of business records generally: only a small percentage of material is readily traceable. However, an important exception to this general scarcity should be noted, in the form of the records of the constituent companies of Upper Clyde Shipbuilders (including John Brown's and Fairfields) which were bought from the liquidator by co-operative purchase in 1973 and entrusted to the custody of the Keeper of the Records of Scotland. The archive, which dates from 1847, includes managerial, financial and production records, as well as technical plans and drawings.

Local transport records, including, for example, those of turnpike trusts,[40] coachbuilders and wheelwrights, material relating to inland navigation, deposited plans and books of reference of railway projects and papers relating to the relations of landowners with railway companies, will all be found in some quantity in county and other local record offices. Some types of transport record are listed in the annual *Sources of Business History in the National Register of Archives,* noted in Chapter Two. Certain types of road transport records seem to be so scarce as, in some cases, to be virtually non-existent. Examples are the records of stage-coach operators and carriers and those of drovers. K. J. Bonser, *The Drovers: Who They Were and How They Went* (Macmillan, 1970), however, shows how much can be recreated even from the limited surviving evidence.

The Thomas Telford Papers, owned by the Institution of Civil Engineers, part of which was listed in detail by the Historical Manuscripts Commission in 1970 (N.R.A. 14021), form a transport archive of national significance, dealing, among other topics, with the Holyhead and South Wales mail road projects and with inland navigation and railways to a lesser extent. A particularly interesting feature is the correspondence relating to the Swedish Gotha Canal on which Telford advised and for which British expertise was crucial. The Telford Papers thus illustrate an important feature of British relations with the Continent in the first half of the 19th century, the export of technical expertise as well as products, a phenomenon to be seen in other surviving archives such as the Dowlais Iron Co. letter books[41] and abroad in archives such as those of Gustav von Mevissen, the Rhineland businessman and railway promoter, in Cologne City Archives.

The motor vehicle was only in its infancy as the century ended, but some valuable archives survive, of which the F. R. Simms papers owned by the Veteran Car Club of Great Britain and deposited in the University of London Library archives department are among the most important. Simms (1863–1944) was an engineer, inventor and entrepreneur; with Bosch he developed electrical ignition for motor vehicles and he was instrumental in introducing Daimler engines and vehicles to the United Kingdom. Small archive groups of his papers are also in the possession of the Royal Automobile Club, of which he was a founder, and the Simms Motor and Electronics Corporation of Finchley. The Veteran Car Club also owns some 200 letters of enquiry addressed to the Yorkshire Motor Car Manufacturing Co. mainly in 1899,[42] which exemplify the kind of commercial and private interest being shown in the motor car at the end of the century.[43]

The motor industry developed in part from the earlier cycle industry. The location of any major surviving 19th-century cycle-manufacturing records is not recorded in the

National Register of Archives, although the records of some
dealers and small 'manufacturers' (in reality, assemblers of
bought-in parts) have survived, and a small quantity of relevant
records of the Birmingham Small Arms Co. as a cycle compo-
nent manufacturer in the late 19th century has survived in the
B.S.A. accession in the Modern Records Centre, University
of Warwick Library. So, too, have some club records and
pre-1900 cycling miscellanea in various repositories.

In conclusion, reference should be made to aviation. True
heavier-than-air flight was not achieved during the century
but ballooning was a feature of the period and there were
projects and experiments of varying degrees of significance, in
particular those of Sir George Cayley (1773-1857). The Royal
Aeronautical Society Library is an important source of pioneer
aviation material. The Science Museum of South Kensington
has rich holdings of *aeronautica,* especially the Penn-Gaskell
Collection[44] which includes, for example, more than a score
of balloon letters sent out from Paris during the siege of
1870-1.

Visual Sources

From correspondence in *Victorian Studies* during 1968[45]
it would appear that finding out about the availability and
location of visual sources for 19th-century history often
proves something of a problem for the researcher. Yet, in
fact, thanks to the invention and development of photography and innovations in printing, the 19th century was
notable for a proliferation of illustrative material and much
of this potential source material has survived.[46] Just how
rich and varied this is may be gathered from the catalogue of
the Arts Council Exhibition, *From Today Painting is Dead*
(Victoria & Albert Museum, 1972), which includes such
little-known items as Barnardo's photographs of waifs and
strays.

It is impossible to list all the relevant sources here. For
publication purposes recourse may be had to such collections
as the *Radio Times* Hulton Picture Library (35 Marylebone
High Street, London, W1M 1AA). Other institutions with
important collections include the Kodak Museum, Harrow, the
Royal Photographic Society, London, the Science Museum,[47]

the Victoria & Albert Museum[48] and, overseas, the Gernsheim Collection in the Humanities Research Center, University of Texas at Austin. The National Portrait Gallery in London is the major centre for iconographic sources and research. (It is interesting to note that its autographic collection, developed by Sir George Scharf, was deposited in the British Museum in 1967/8: Add. MSS. 54224-6.) The National Monuments Record (England) (Fortress House, 23 Savile Row, London, W1X 1AB) has, in addition to modern photographs taken for record purposes, original 19th-century material on buildings.[49] The Museum of English Rural Life at Reading University possesses a unique stock of agricultural and rural scenes. Many county record offices and local libraries have photographic collections which may include 19th-century views, often significant as evidence for social as well as architectural history.[50] Then there are individual photographic archives, such as those of Frank M. Sutcliffe of Whitby, Charles Emeny of Felixstowe, S. W. A. Newton (now at Leïcester Museum), who recorded the making of the Great Central Railway, the last Victorian main line, or Samuel Smith (1802–92), the East Anglian calotype photographer.[51]

Printed and engraved items, such as bill- and letter-heads, catalogues, leaflets, handbills, tickets and a variety of other proforma, can be of considerable value, both as source material in their own right and as illustrations, although allowance may need to be made for artistic licence, for instance in the depiction of buildings. Such collections are discussed in Chapter Eight. M. W. Barley, *A Guide to British Topographical Collections* (London, Council for British Archaeology, 1974) covers drawings, prints and photographs.

It should not be forgotten that many 19th-century artefacts, both large and small, the products of crafts and of heavy industry, survive in the national, local and specialist museums of the United Kingdom. They constitute an original source in their own right for many branches of history and should be incorporated in any truly comprehensive study. One of the benefits derived by business and technological history from industrial archaeology[52] has been a trend towards integrating the physical evidence of sites and artefacts with manuscript, printed and photographic sources to produce rounded studies which, at their best, are also interdisciplinary.

Some Wider Themes

A short guide cannot hope to do justice to the wide range of Victorian activity, both corporate and individual, which would fall within the scope of social history in its broadest definition. In these concluding remarks we can do no more than indicate some of the record possibilities for a few other fields of research.

Some, but probably a minority, of the charitable and humanitarian organisations which have survived into the late 20th century will have records in reasonable order and at least partially open for research. For example, for Sabbatarianism, the Lord's Day Observance Society (55 Fleet Street, London, E.C.4) holds surviving minutes, printed reports and journals, and some 19th-century records of bodies united with it. For the others, library holdings of their reports and other publications will have to provide a substitute, perhaps supplemented by the personal papers of significant supporters. Branch records and other evidence of local activity might be found in local record offices and the National Register of Archives' Subject Index should always be consulted.

The phenomenon of phrenology as, in its practitioners' eyes, a practical science leading to the rational improvement of society, does not immediately spring to mind when considering Victorian social reformers. The concern of phrenologists such as Andrew and George Combe[53] with moral and social issues is, however, convincingly demonstrated by David de Giustino in a recent article.[54] A more obvious well-spring of reform, Utilitarianism, is exemplified by the Bentham and John Stuart Mill publishing projects[55] and the Bentham papers in the Library of University College, London, and the Mill-Taylor papers in the British Library of Political and Economic Science.

In some cases publication based on recent research will provide an introduction both to the subject and to its sources, as Brian Harrison's significant *Drink and the Victorians: the Temperance Question in England, 1815–1872* (Faber, 1971) does for temperance.[56] Funding by the Social Science Research Council initiated in late 1972 the listing of the manuscript holdings of the Fawcett Library (27 Wilfred Street, London, S.W.1), which are central to any study of feminism, and it is hoped that the archives of other special-purpose bodies will similarly be made accessible. For pacifism, the correspondence of Henry Richard, secretary of the Peace Society, is in the National Library of Wales, the Society itself still continues in London, and the manuscript holdings of the Library of the Society of Friends (Friends House, Euston Road, London, N.W.1) would prove rewarding for this and other causes.[57] Another aspect of humanitarianism is represented by the archives of the Anti-Slavery Society in Rhodes House Library, South Parks Road, Oxford (N.R.A. 1095).

Concepts of conservation, town and country planning and popular rights come together in the records of the Commons, Open Spaces and Footpaths Preservation Society (founded in 1865 as the Commons Preservation Society) and earlier and allied societies in the House of Lords Record Office. These include papers dealing with such important issues as the preservation of Epping Forest and Ken Wood and the extension of Hampstead Heath. It is interesting to note that supplementary material, correspondence on thinnings in Epping Forest, 1894-5, will be found in the Meldola Papers in the Passmore Edwards Museum (Romford Road, Stratford, London, E.15).[58]

Much work remains to be done in locating and listing the wide range of sources for social history, but many archivists and librarians are now alive to the problems and the opportunities and the researcher is in a much better position than he would have been even a decade ago. This is particularly true as far as published guides are concerned. Thus, as this work went to press, two guides to specialised areas of research appeared: R. P. Sturges, *Economists' Papers, 1750-1950* (Macmillan, 1975), which lists manuscript sources for the history of British economic thought, and C. J. Kitching, *The Central Records of the Church* (London, Church Information Office, 1976), the Appendix to which includes details of numerous Anglican organisations' records. Researchers themselves can sometimes play a useful role as agents in the field, putting harassed administrators in touch with an appropriate repository or archive organisation and thereby solving an archive problem to everyone's advantage.

ORGANISATION AND DESCRIPTION OF MATERIALS

Terminology and Arrangement

All research students should have some acquaintance with the specialised terminology and general practice current in archive administration. The term *archives* itself tends to be used imprecisely and confusingly to denote both a *repository* where manuscripts are kept and the manuscripts themselves, which in many cases are not archives in the true sense of the word.

Archives may be broadly defined as the non-current working papers of an individual or institution. In the strictest interpretation of the word they should remain in the unbroken custody of their creator or his successors.[1] They are, of course, unlikely to comprise all the correspondence and papers created by the person or body concerned, since *weeding*—the discarding of more ephemeral and less important material—almost inevitably occurs as an archive accumulates. Moreover, most individuals and, in the 19th century, many institutions do not keep copies of the letters they write, the originals of which will therefore have to be sought amongst the archives of their correspondents.

In the case of an individual, the term *personal papers* or, more simply, *papers* are often used to denote what is, in fact, an archive. The German term *Nachlass* (plural *Nachlässe*) is a useful alternative to denote manuscripts left by an individual on his death, and can cover both archive and collected material.

It is important to distinguish between letters received, *in-letters,* of which an individual's *Nachlass* will normally be composed, and letters despatched, *out-letters,* which in a true archive should be present only in the form of copies. In individuals' *Nachlässe* it is unusual to find copies of more than a few isolated letters considered by the writer to be of special significance, but business or institutional archives may contain complete series of copy out-letters, perhaps in the form of wet-copy flimsy letter-books. However, it was not uncommon in the 19th century for the relatives of one recently deceased to solicit from friends and acquaintances any original letters from the deceased, usually with the intention of compiling some kind of memorial volume including extracts from the correspondence.[2] The originals of such collected letters might then be added to the *Nachlass*.

The alternative to an archive is some form of *artificial collection,* the adjective being appended to stress the contrast between collected papers and those which have accumulated naturally as an archive. An *autograph collection* of letters collected for their association with prominent persons is the most obvious example, but it will sometimes be the case that what at first sight appears, for example, to be a straightforward business archive is in reality a collection, consisting of fragmentary archives to which collected material has been added, perhaps by a keen public relations department.

An autograph collection, properly so-called, consists of a heterogeneous accumulation of letters to different addressees and possibly other autograph items, the only common factor of which is that they have all been collected by one person or family. What appears superficially to be an autograph collection may on closer inspection prove to be a selection of letters from an individual's in-letters, made by him or his family for autograph purposes. Such an *autograph selection,* if we may coin the phrase, will have a greater coherence and significance than a mere collection. Sometimes both features will be combined, as in the original deposit of Field Marshal Lord Wolseley's papers in Hove Central Library. The bulk of the correspondence sequence consists of letters to Wolseley kept for the prominence of their writers, or the interest of their contents. To these have been added single letters or small groups deliberately acquired as autographs—for instance, a group of letters to Archdeacon Sinclair.

Some reference to the significance of autograph collections and problems they present has been made in Chapter One. A further factor to be considered by the researcher is the possible existence of a number of fragmented *Nachlässe* within an autograph collection. Thus letters received by Brown, Jones, Smith, Taylor and Walker may be inter-filed with many other single letters in one single alphabetical sequence by writer. This may effectively serve to disguise the existence of such coherent groups of in-letters. The possibility is stressed here not as a pedantic point of archival expertise, but because the individual letters making up a *Nachlass* gain in significance from being seen as part of a whole, in relation to the other correspondence of their recipient, and it is only when a group of related letters is thus identified that the recipient himself can feature in a meaningful way in any guide to the manuscripts concerned. (The problem of bringing together information on correspondents who feature in a number of such *Nachlässe* can be simply solved by a card-index.) The subconscious drawing of a false analogy between the writers of individual letters and the authors of books may in the past have been responsible for the creation of such misleading single alphabetical sequences of letters, irrespective of their recipients. The basic error in such an arrangement lies in choosing the wrong unit, the letter, rather than the group of letters with a common addressee.

A contrast has been made between 'social' letters kept for their autograph interest and those with important subject content. This is in many ways a valid distinction, but, without advocating an archival or historical objective of total recall, the value of the 'social' letters for any study of an individual's nexus of relationships, personal, social, or professional, should not be overlooked.

Considerable attention has been paid to autograph collections in this guide because it is the conviction, based on experience, of its compilers, that much important source material for 19th-century studies still lies fallow in such collections. Autograph collecting is still very much alive, as may be seen from Ray Rawlins, *Four Hundred Years of British Autographs: A Collector's Guide* (Dent, 1970). The first chapter of this book —'Autograph collecting: a hobby and a serious study'—casts interesting light on the attitudes of collectors. The pursuit, however, was perhaps a particularly Victorian phenomenon, the product of educated upper-class girls and women with time on their hands and a wide acquaintanceship through the head of the household and male relatives. The greatest collectors were, of course, men of wealth with scholarly interests, as well as a touch of the collecting mania. Their activities are described with great sympathy and erudition by A. N. L. Munby in *The Cult of the Autograph Letter in England* (Athlone, 1962) which is essential reading for this subject.[3]

Some collectors of autographs have published catalogues of their collections. Richard D. Altick has indicated the value of such catalogues to literary biographers and editors of correspondence. In his very useful article, 'A neglected source of literary biography',[4] Altick cites as an example *A Catalogue of the Collection of Autographs Formed by Julius Dreer* (2 vols., Philadelphia, 1890), which provides texts or summaries of some letters, including items written by Keats and Dickens. Other sources of information about autographs include: the books of anecdotes written by collectors, which often include texts of letters; old sale catalogues of autograph collections; periodicals such as *The Autograph Album, L'Autograph* and *The Autograph Mirror*; and books of facsimiles, of which many were issued in England and on the Continent in the 19th century.

Despite the existence of some catalogues and anecdotal guides, however, researchers must resign themselves to the idea that much of this material will remain unknown and inaccessible in private hands, and that collections in libraries and other repositories are not always given adequate cataloguing treatment. As an illustration of this the student should consult the long and frank article by M. A. Smith on 'Autograph letters' in *Manchester Review*.[5] This article briefly outlines the general problems associated with autograph letters and then examines in some detail the collections in the Manchester public libraries.

Both archives and collections of manuscripts are *primary sources*. By *secondary sources* are understood such items as collections of press-cuttings and articles on a subject, rather than the original manuscripts which form the basic raw material for its study. The term *manuscripts* (MSS.) is, in general use, not restricted to hand-written documents, but is understood to cover typewritten and duplicated items and printed or photographic material found as an integral part of an archive or collection.

There is much useful information in J. H. Hodson, *The Administration of Archives* (Oxford, Pergamon, 1972), though this is primarily a book written by an archivist for fellow archivists rather than for research workers, and it is likely to annoy the former by its habit of quoting authors' statements of different dates against themselves. However, it includes a valuable critique of the 'mystique of custody' propagated by Sir Hilary Jenkinson in his definition of archives, and it puts in perspective the relationship of administrative and historical need in the preservation of archives: 'it is accident plus the wishes of researchers . . . which ultimately have preserved medieval and modern records'. This is probably true in more cases than archivists would care to admit. Research students will find the section on the description of archives (pp. 129-35) particularly helpful.

Philip C. Brooks, *Research in Archives: The use of Unpublished Primary Sources* (Chicago, University Press, 1969), although of some value, is strongly biased to the discussion of American practice.

Printed Ephemera

The important body of material comprised under this heading includes such varied items as trade cards, bill heads, handbills, posters, leaflets, postcards and tickets. Responsibility for this material falls uneasily between the librarian and the archivist. In fact, it has tended to be ignored by both, as well as by the historian. This is to be regretted, for much valuable source material, for the social historian in particular, may be found within such accumulation. Information on individuals in many walks of life may be found in such items as the printed *curriculum vitae* or the notices of public lectures which serve as records of engagements of preachers, politicians and other public figures.

There is growing recognition of the value of printed ephemera. Significant early studies included Sir Ambrose Heal, *London Tradesmen's Cards of the XVIII Century: An Account of their Origin and Use* (Batsford, 1925, reprinted

Dover/Constable, 1968) and J. Ballinger, *Gleanings from a Printer's File* (Aberystwyth, National Library of Wales, 1928), based on a study of the *Tivyside Advertiser*. More recently, John Lewis has provided a lavishly-illustrated guide to the development of many kinds of material in his *Printed Ephemera: The Changing Uses of Type and Letterforms in English and American Printing* (Ipswich, W. S. Cowell, 1962, reprinted Faber, 1969). M. Twyman and W. Rollinson, *John Soulby, Printer, Ulverston* (Reading, University Museum of English Rural Life, 1966) is an excellent study of a local printer and an examination of the evidential value of his material. *Scientific Trade Cards in The Science Museum Collection,* by H. R. Calvert (H.M.S.O., 1971) is a catalogue which shows the value of ephemera in a specific subject field.

In 1968 the Bodleian Library acquired a magnificent collection of printed ephemera which had been built up by John Johnson during his career as Printer to the University of Oxford and after his retirement in 1946. When the collection was transferred to the Bodleian Library it consisted of some 2,500 folio boxes of items as well as large folders, cabinets of drawers and many hundreds of volumes. Johnson deliberately set out to collect the sort of material which libraries would reject, even if it were offered as a gift. The philosophy behind his collection and the success he achieved were admirably indicated by an exhibition in the Bodleian in 1971. *The John Johnson Collection: Catalogue of an Exhibition* (Oxford, Bodleian Library, 1971) includes very informative notes on the items selected for exhibition and a most interesting introduction—'John Johnson and his collection of printed ephemera'— by Michael L. Turner, the curator of the collection.

In the past, printed ephemera have been most frequently collected and studied by historians of printing. An indication that this class of material is now recognised as of interest to a much wider range of students is given by the appearance of relevant articles and notes in *Business Archives*.[6] Recently. John E. Pemberton, then of the University of Warwick, compiled a report emphasising the value of printed ephemera to social scientists. *The National Provision of Printed Ephemera in the Social Sciences: A Report Prepared for the Social Science and Government Committee of the Social Science Research Council*

(Coventry, University of Warwick Library, 1971) recommends as a matter of urgency the establishment of a National Documents Library to house printed ephemera in the social sciences. This library, which should have equivalent status to the Official Publications Library in the British Library Reference Division, should assemble the printed ephemera at present scattered in the British Library and should collect new British material under the Copyright Act. It is difficult to envisage these recommendations being implemented in the foreseeable future, but there can be little doubt that Pemberton's advocacy has stimulated existing institutions to make fuller provision for the collection and cataloguing of this type of material.[7]

Archive Lists

Formerly listing frequently took the form of a *calendar,* a chronologically arranged series of detailed descriptions of, or extracts from, individual documents. In face of the modern pressure on repository staffs, and in view of the relative cheapness and ease of modern copying methods, calendars have generally given way to *summary lists,* or in some cases to *descriptive lists*, which in many ways resemble calendars, but lack some of their fullness of detail. A typical entry in a summary list might read:

> 26/1-50 1850-1   Letters accompanying subscriptions to New School building fund, mainly addressed to John Wilson.

A *descriptive list* is made up of descriptions of individual items, similar to the following:

> 26/14   1850 Jan 23   Thos. Brown, Braintree, to John Wilson: sends subscription and comments on nonconformist situation in Braintree and on decline of malting industry there.

In practice, many lists are a mixture of summary and descriptive, especially if a wide range of documents of varying significance is being dealt with. The National Register of Archives' list of the Locker-Lampson MSS. (N.R.A. 12288) is an example of a descriptive list, whereas the same organisation's list of the archives of New College, London (N.R.A.

13042) is a mixed list, made up of summary descriptions of some groups and detailed descriptions of individual manuscripts in others.

Manuscripts deposited in a repository will receive an *accession number* (e.g., Acc. 234) at the time of deposit. This will form part of a running series recorded in an accessions register, which is the repository's basic record of its holdings. On listing, each deposit may also be given a classification. Thus, for example, deposited documents of the Baker family would, under some systems, receive the code DD/BA. Each document within deposit DD/BA would then be given an individual number, possibly with a code letter standard to the repository signifying the type of document and its place within the groups into which the deposit might be divided (e.g., those relating to title to property, to estate administration, to family or to personal affairs). The correct citation of the individual manuscript would then be, for example, DD/BA: T 54, comprising the archive classification and the document classification and number. An alternative system is to have bundle or group document numbers following the deposit code, as DD/BA: 26/54.

Researchers using the National Register of Archives should realise that the N.R.A. report number (the filing number of a list in the N.R.A. series) has no relevance outside the National Register and should not be quoted to repositories. It may, however, usefully be cited in footnotes, e.g., as N.R.A. 12345.

Some Common Abbreviations and Conventions

A large number of the abbreviations frequently used by archivists are self-explanatory. The student will encounter no difficulty in interpreting such abbreviations as a/c bk., corres., ltr., min. bk., pprs. The exact meaning of the following generally accepted abbreviations should, however, be carefully noted:

a.c.s. (plural a.cs.s.) autograph card signed.
a.d.s. (plural a.ds.s.) autograph document signed
a.l.s. (plural a.ls.s.) autograph letter signed.
a.ms.s. (plural a.mss. s.) autograph manuscript signed
a.n.s. (plural a.ns.s.) autograph note signed

All the abbreviations listed here refer to items which are entirely in the handwriting of the signer. A signed document which is printed or typed or is written in the hand of another person than the signer is often described as d.s. (plural ds.s.). Similarly, a signed letter which is printed or typed or is written in the hand of a person other than the signer is described as l.s. (plural ls.s.).

It is important to be careful when citing dates in lists of papers and documents. The abbreviation n.d. indicates that no date is given and none has been deduced by the archivist. A date in square brackets—e.g. [1864]—indicates that, although the date is not given on the document, the archivist has discovered a reliable date from internal or other evidence. A date in square brackets with a query—e.g. [1864?]—indicates that the archivist has assumed a date which is probably correct, but for which there is not sufficient evidence to warrant a certain attribution.

Further information about abbreviations and conventions can be found in Mary C. Turner, *The Bookman's Glossary* (New York, Bowker, 1961). Terms in English, French, German, Spanish, Italian, and Dutch are listed in *Elsevier's Lexicon of Archive Terminology,* compiled by a committee of the International Council on Archives (Amsterdam, Elsevier, 1964).

SOME PRACTICAL HINTS

ALL RESEARCH STUDENTS should equip themselves with an appropriate guide to research methods. G. Kitson Clark, *Guide for Students Working on Historical Subjects* (2nd ed., C.U.P., 1968) is a brief introduction which includes an enormous amount of excellent advice on the preparation and presentation of historical research. A similar work for literary students, George Watson, *The Literary Thesis: A Guide to Research* (Longman, 1970) includes a useful short chapter on the location and use of literary manuscripts.

General guides such as these include incidental advice on the use of unpublished sources. It is particularly important to remember, however, that, unlike books, unpublished materials are unique items and should therefore be treated with exceptional care. Common sense as well as the rules of record offices and manuscript departments require that, when working on such materials, students should use a pencil, not a fountain or ball-point pen, for their note-taking or transcribing. The documents should be kept free of other papers, books or objects and away from any liquids. Because of their fragile nature the reader should avoid leaning on them. Every care should be taken to avoid creasing or tearing the documents when removing them from or replacing them in their folders or envelopes. No smoking is, of course, an inflexible rule for all work on or contact with manuscripts.

When working on unsorted and unlisted manuscripts it is very important to preserve their original sequence. This may have significance when the archivist is dating and assessing individual items which may only be intelligible within the context of the original sequence of documents of which they form a part. It is for this reason that many repositories do not allow research work on unprocessed deposits. Should any annotation seem necessary, pencilled slips should be carefully attached to the documents in question with brass or plastic paper clips.

Although archivists, librarians and curators of collections are eager to help the student, it is important to be as courteous and thoughtful as possible in seeking their assistance. If the institution issues a guide to the use of its collections, this should be carefully studied before using the collection. The student should always give advance notice of his desire to use a collection; he should write, setting out as clearly as he can the nature of his interest and the aims of his search. It cannot be too strongly emphasised that it is no use simply turning up unannounced and expecting to receive immediate attention. The nature of archive collections themselves and the fact that most archives are short-staffed and their staff consequently overworked means that such action is certain to bring frustration. Requests to private owners, of course, should always be made by letter. It must be clearly recognised that such owners are conferring a favour, not a right, in allowing use of their holdings.

Enquiries about copying facilities must be made to the institution holding the materials. Where photocopying services can be employed these will obviously save time and ensure greater accuracy than the process of manual transcription which is always open to error. Where transcription is used the student must take great pains in checking to ensure that his work is accurate.

Sometimes the fragile state of certain documents will prevent their being made available for consultation by students. In such cases the archivist's primary duty is the preservation of the materials which have been deposited in his care. If possible, photocopies will be supplied for use in place of the original documents.

Although the student may encounter difficulties because of the physical state of the documents he wishes to consult, he is much more likely to be frustrated by limitations placed on his use of the actual contents of his sources. Private collections, of course, are often subject to the dictates of their owners. The use of documents in public collections may be limited by the terms of a bequest or by the stipulations of the depositor. As an extreme example of such a restriction, the important collection of Tennyson manuscripts placed in Trinity College, Cambridge, by Hallam, Lord Tennyson, in 1924 was deposited subject to the condition that they might not be copied or quoted *in perpetuity*. Happily, largely as a result of the influence of the present Lord Tennyson and Sir Charles Tennyson, this restriction was relaxed in 1969, though unfortunately not until after the publication of Christopher Ricks's major edition of *The Poems of Tennyson* (Longman, 1969).

Questions of copyright should be carefully checked before manuscript material is published. Proper observance of copyright law is the responsibility of the student himself and not of the institution which holds the material. It is important to remember that copyright belongs to the author of the material and normally passes to his heirs, though he can, in fact, dispose of it by gift or sale as he wishes. Thus the copyright of letters received from other people belongs not to the recipient, but to the writers of the letters and their heirs.

Questions about the publication of manuscript material in private hands must be referred to the owner of the copyright. If the owner of copyright cannot be found, unpublished materials in repositories may usually be published at a time which falls 50 years after the death of the author and 100 years after the writing of the work. There is a useful short discussion of this provision in 'Notes on the history of English copyright', by Sir Frank Mackinnon, which forms Appendix II to *The Oxford Companion to English Literature,* compiled by Sir Paul Harvey (4th ed., revised by Dorothy Eagle, Oxford, Clarendon Press, 1967). The whole subject of copyright of manuscript materials is complicated. In many cases the student will, in fact, find it impossible to locate the owner of the copyright. If he wishes to use unpublished material extensively, however, whether in a thesis or a published work, he would be well advised to make the effort to obtain the necessary permission.

REFERENCES

Chapter 1.

1. See also M. H. Adler, *The Writing Machine* (Allen & Unwin, 1973); W. A. Beeching, *Century of the Typewriter* (Heinemann, 1974); J. I. Whalley, *Writing Implements & Accessories: from the Roman Stylus to the Typewritter* (Newton Abbot, David & Charles, 1975).

2. *Bank of England Quarterly Bulletin*, Vol. 12 (1972), pp. 208-12.

3. Some of the material in this book was first published in 'Copying methods past and present', *Proceedings of the Royal Institution of Great Britain*, Vol. 41 (1966), pp. 270-309.

Chapter 2.

1. An important group of articles appeared in *Journal of the Society of Archivists*, Vol. 3 (April 1969), pp. 441-69.

2. Before 1973 this was entitled *List of Accessions to Repositories*.

3. *Indexer*, Vol. 5 (1967), pp. 159-68.

4. It is not normally possible to purchase copies of the lists which are filed in the National Register of Archives, but a limited number of copies of both the *Locker-Lampson* and the *New College, London*, lists are available. Details of prices may be obtained direct from the Commission.

5. *Secretary's Report to the Commissioners, 1974-75*, pp. 5, 15.

Chapter 3.

1. See Lionel Bell, 'The new Public Record Office at Kew', *Journal of the Society of Archivists*, Vol. 5, No. 1 (April, 1974), pp. 1-7.

2. See Royal Commission on Historical Manuscripts, *Report of the Secretary to the Commissioners, 1968-69* (H.M.S.O., 1969), pp. 47-50.

3. There is a useful note by the Keeper of Public Records on the records of nationalised industries in *The Preservation of Technological Material: Report and Recommendations of a Working Party of the Standing Commission on Museums and Galleries* (H.M.S.O., 1971), pp. 36-8.

4. See *Reports of the Keeper of Public Records for 1971* (H.M.S.O., 1972), and for 1972 (H.M.S.O., 1973).

5. Maurice Bond has also written a useful booklet, *The Records of Parliament: A Guide for Genealogists and Local Historians* (Phillimore, 1964).

6. In late 1973 the British Museum Library with related departments, such as the Department of Manuscripts, State Paper Room, and Newspaper Library, were hived off from the British Museum to become the British Library.

7. See, for example, *Report of the Deputy Keeper of the Records for the Years 1960–1965* (Belfast, H.M.S.O., 1968).

8. See *Catalogue of Publications Issued and In Preparation 1928–1966* (Dublin, Irish Stationery Office, 1966). A survey of business records in Eire organised by the Commission began in 1970.

Chapter 4.

1. It should be noted that West Yorkshire Metropolitan County Archives were set up under the reorganisation of local government in April 1974 and include the records of the former West Riding Registry of Deeds. One nationwide development to note is the absorbing of some former borough record offices into the county records system as area offices.

2. East and West Suffolk became one administrative county in 1974.

3. For note of retitling, see p. 7.

4. See report of the British Records Association annual conference 1972, in *Archives*, Vol. 11, No. 49 (Spring 1973), pp. 27–32; also B.R.A. Memorandum No. 21, *Records of District Councils* (1974).

Chapter 5.

1. *Aslib Directory*, introduction, p. vii.

2. His papers were deposited in the University of London Library archives department in May 1972. There is a typescript handlist of the unpublished manuscripts (MS. 804).

Chapter 6.

1. 1. *Archives*, Vol. 9 (1970), pp. 121–9.

Chapter 7.

1. A large number of drawings from the Museum's collections were included in the autumn 1973 exhibition devoted to Victorian secular buildings. They are described in the catalogue *Marble Halls*, by John Physick and M. Darby. The Victoria & Albert Museum's holdings for theatre history which include the Enthoven and Beard Collections, together with the British Theatre Museum collections (formerly in Leighton House, W.14) are to form the nucleus of the new Theatre Museum, planned as a separate branch museum of the V. & A. This is now to be housed in Covent Garden in the late 1970s, and not in Somerset House as originally planned. Other theatre sources include the British Library and the private Mander & Mitchenson Theatre Collection in Sydenham.

2. Published guides are available, e.g., *Catalogue of the Morris Collection* (2nd ed., The Gallery, 1969).

3. See, for example, C. Booker and Candida Lycett-Green, *Goodbye London* (Fontana/Collins, 1973), which illustrates a large proportion of Victorian buildings amongst those threatened by redevelopment.

4. See a note by R. A. Storey, 'Evidence from buildings', in *Urban History Newsletter*, No. 13 (December, 1969). This useful periodical has now been succeeded by the annual *Urban History Yearbook* (Leicester, University Press, 1974–), also edited by H. J. Dyos.

5. Other surveys of business records which should be mentioned are: D. C. M. Platt, *Latin America: Business Archives in the United Kingdom* (1965), a duplicated part of the *Guide to Manuscript Sources in the British Isles for the History of Latin America and the Caribbean*, edited by P. Walne (Oxford University Press, 1973); and E. J. R. Owen and F. Dux, *List of the Location of Records Belonging to British Businessmen Active in the Middle East, 1800-1950* (Oxford, St. Antony's College, 1972).

6. *Studies in Scottish Business History*, ed. P.L. Payne (Cass, 1967) should also be noted.

7. *Historical Farm Records: A Summary Guide to Manuscripts & other Material in the University Library Collected by the Institute of Agricultural History & the Museum of English Rural Life*, J.A. Edwards (Reading, University Library, 1973).

8. For a published example see *The Oxley Parker Papers* (from the letters and diaries of an Essex family of land agents in the 19th century), by J. Oxley Parker (Colchester, Benham & Co., 1964), based on correspondence and diaries largely in Essex Record Office. Reading University has also surveyed and collected records of agricultural engineering: see, for example, D. R. Grace and D. C. Phillips, *Ransomes of Ipswich: A History of the Firm and Guide to its Records* (Reading, Institute of Agricultural History, 1975). A number of county record offices, such as Essex, Hertfordshire and Kent, publish catalogues of manuscript estate and other local maps in their custody.

9. As an indication of the type of material available, see Angela Black, *Guide to Education Records in the County Record Office, Cambridge* (Cambridge, Cambridgeshire and I. of Ely C.C., 1972).

10. H. Peek and C. M. Hall, *The Archives of the University of Cambridge: An Historical Introduction* (C.U.P., 1962).

11. Ed. C. H. S. Fifoot (Selden Society, 1965).

12. See, for example, the meticulously kept notebooks of the metallurgist, C. H. Desch, F.R.S. (1874-1958), from Birkbeck School, Kingsland, the City and Guilds Technical College, Finsbury, private study while in employment, and from Würzburg University, among the Desch Papers in Sheffield University Library (CHD. 3/1-56).

13. See below, p. 50.

14. See, for example, *Records of the Colonial and Dominions Office*, by R. B. Pugh (H.M.S.O., 1964: P.R.O. Handbooks, No. 3).

15. See S. C. Sutton, *A Guide to the India Office Library with a Note on the India Office Records* (2nd ed. revised, H.M.S.O., 1968).

16. *Manuscript Catalogue of the Library of the Royal Commonwealth Society*, ed. D. H. Simpson (Mansell, 1975).

16a. In 1971 the Tennyson Society commenced publication of a three-volume work, *Tennyson in Lincoln: A Catalogue of the Collections in the*

Research Centre, compiled by Nancie Campbell. Two volumes have so far been published. The *Catalogue of the Suzannet Charles Dickens Collection,* ed. M. Slater, was published by Sotheby Parke Bernet and the Trustees of Dickens House in 1975.

17. *Forster Collection. A Catalogue of the Paintings, Manuscripts, Autograph Letters, Pamphlets, etc. Bequeathed by John Forster,* compiled by R. F. Sketchley (H.M.S.O., for Victoria & Albert Museum, 1893).

18. The *terminus a quo* of the Imperial War Museum is August 1914, and the holdings of the Military Archive of King's College, London, are 20th-century.

19. For National Maritime Museum see K. F. Lindsay-MacDougall, *Guide to the Manuscripts at the National Maritime Museum* (Greenwich, The Museum, 1960). The publications of the Navy Records Society are in some cases relevant to the 19th century and the possibility of sources elsewhere should not be overlooked, for example, the Goodrich Papers in the Science Museum, illuminating an aspect of naval technology: K. R. Gilbert, *The Portsmouth Blockmaking Machinery* (H.M.S.O., 1965).

20. See *Report of the Secretary to the Commissioners 1968–69* (H.M.S.O., 1969), pp. 47–50.

21. See *The Gladstone Papers* (British Museum, 1953), and the Historical Manuscripts Commission series of *Prime Ministers' Papers,* ed. John Brooke, noted in Chapter Two.

22. Housed in the Gladstone Memorial Library, Hawarden, and being listed by the Flintshire County Record Office (see Chapter 4).

23. See *The Gladstone Diaries,* ed. M. R. D. Foot & H. C. G. Matthew (4 vols., Oxford, Clarendon Press, 1968, 1974).

24. For an introduction to the extremely important holdings of the British Library of Political and Economic Science, housed in the London School of Economics, see *Outline of the Resources of the Library* (The Library, 1972). The *Nachlässe* of George Holyoake and George Howell in the Bishopsgate Institute (230 Bishopsgate, London, E.C.2) should not be overlooked; an *Index* to the Howell Correspondence, 1864–1910, was issued by the Institute in 1973. The latter includes personal diaries of Ernest Jones, the Chartist, Reform League papers, and the International Working Men's Association minutes, 1866–69. The Modern Records Centre established in the University of Warwick Library in October 1973 has already received numerous accessions of relevance to 19th-century labour history, such as minutes of the predecessors of the National Graphical Association and its London Region. Details of the Centre's accessions are given in its quarterly *Information Bulletin* (No. 1, April 1974–   ). A *Guide* is to be published in late 1977.

25. See John R. Vincent's later book, *Pollbooks: How Victorians Voted* (C.U.P., 1967), and C. R. Dod, *Electoral Facts 1832-1853,* ed. H. J. Hanham, with bibliography of pollbook locations (Brighton, Harvester Press, 1972). Also C. Cook & B. Keith, *British Historical Facts: 1830-1900* (Macmillan, 1975).

26. A good example is found in *A Victorian M.P. and his Constituents,* ed. B. S. Trinder (Banbury, Banbury Historical Society, 1969)

which prints correspondence of Henry Tancred, M.P., to his agents, the Banbury solicitors, John and William Munton, 1841–59.

27. G. A. Godding, jr., *The Universal Postal Union: Co-ordinator of the International Mails* (New York, University Press, 1964).

28. New College, London Archives, L.21/14.

29. The first railway sorting carriages were introduced in 1838, and a variety of cancellations developed to indicate mail handled on a Sorting Tender or Travelling Post Office. 'R.S.O.', sometimes found on country-house stationery, denoted a railway sub-office receiving mail direct from the sorting carriages.

30. See, for example, A. G. Rigo de Righi's booklet on the De La Rue philatelic archive now in the National Postal Museum, *Postage Stamps of De La Rue* (National Postal Museum, [1973]).

31. As one example we may cite the decline in messenger traffic between the City and the docks, travelling on the Blackwall trains from Fenchurch Street, which is referred to by A. A. Jackson in his study of *London's Termini* (Newton Abbot, David & Charles, 1969).

32. For a useful account see B. Maidment, 'Author and publisher—John Ruskin and George Allen, 1890–1900', *Business Archives*, No. 36 (June 1972), pp. 21–32.

33. As an example of the kind of use which can be made of a publisher's archive see *Joseph Conrad: Letters to William Blackwood and David S. Meldrum*, ed. W. Blackburn (Durham, N.C., Duke University Press, 1958). The sequence begins with Conrad's break with his first publisher in 1897.

34. For a description of the Macmillan archives see *British Museum Quarterly*, Vol. 36, 3–4 (1972).

35. *The Waterloo Directory of Victorian Periodicals 1824–1900: Phase I* (Waterloo, Wilfrid Laurier University Press, for University of Waterloo, 1976).

36. *Archives*, Vol. 6 (1964), pp. 235–8.

37. The project was announced in a short article by the late Sir Harold Hartley in *New Scientist*, 22 February 1968, p. 422.

38. This work was published as Vol. 4, No. 3 of the *Bulletin* of the British Museum (Natural History).

39. *Journal of Transport History*, Vol. 1 (1954), pp. 155–69.

40. W. Albert, *The Turnpike Road System in England 1663–1840* (C.U.P., 1972) is based on and lists many of these records.

41. Cf. *Iron in the Making: Dowlais Iron Company Letters, 1782–1860*, ed. Madeleine Elsas (Cardiff, Glamorgan County Council, 1960).

42. Most of this material has been listed in detail by the Historical Manuscripts Commission. See, for example, *Bulletin* of the National Register of Archives, Nos. 13 and 14 (1964 and 1967).

43. There are three excellent guides to the welter of small firms beginning to spring up by the end of the century: G. R. Doyle and G. N. Georgano, *The World's Automobiles* (Temple Press, 1963); E. Tragatsch, *The World's Motorcycles 1844–1963* (Temple Press, 1964); G. N.

Georgano, *The World's Commercial Vehicles 1830–1964* (Temple Press, 1965).

44. Cf. W. T. O'Dea, *Aeronautica* (H.M.S.O., 1966). A 'Science Museum Illustrated Booklet'.

45. *Victorian Studies*, Vol. 11 (1968), pp. 423, 616.

46. One important published historical source, the 19th-century volumes of the *Illustrated London News*, has recently been reproduced on microfiche (Vols. 1–145, 1842–1914. Washington, Microcard Editions).

47. D. B. Thomas, *The Science Museum Photography Collection* (H.M.S.O., 1969).

48. See, for example, *Collecting & Valuing Old Photographs*, by Peter Castle, curator of photographs at the V. & A. (Garnstone Press, 1973).

49. For a description of its recent work, see *National Monuments Record (England) Report 1966–1971* (Royal Commission on Historical Monuments [England] [1973]).

50. The lack of a *national* photographic collection began to be discussed in the *Sunday Times* in October 1972. The whole question was aired and developments chronicled in the same newspaper between October 1972 and April 1973 and the *Sunday Times* launched a successful appeal for the compilation of a National Photographic Record. A modern wing of the National Portrait Gallery, concentrating on film and photographic material, was opened at Carlton House Terrace, London, in April 1974 with an exhibition of Sir Benjamin Stone's photographs.

51. See *In and Around Victorian Felixstowe*, ed. C. Corker (Felixstowe, A. C. Phillips, 1972); *The Last Main Line*, ed. R. D. Abbott (Leicester, Leicester Museums, 1960). Two major collections of Smith's paper negatives and contemporary prints are in the Wisbech & Fenland Museum and the Kodak Museum. The Stone Collection is in Birmingham Public Library.

52. See *Industrial Archaeology* (Newton Abbot, David & Charles). This periodical continued the *Journal of Industrial Archaeology* (1964–). R. A. Buchanan, *Industrial Archaeology in Britain* (Penguin, 1972) provides a useful introduction, which may be supplemented by A. Raistrick, *Industrial Archaeology* (Eyre Methuen, 1972, reprinted St. Albans, Paladin, 1973).

53. The Combe papers are in the National Library of Scotland.

54. 'Reforming the commonwealth of thieves: British phrenologists and Australia', *Victorian Studies*, Vol. 15 (1972), pp. 439–61.

55. *The Collected Works of Jeremy Bentham*, ed. J. H. Burns (Athlone Press, 1968–) and *Collected Works of John Stuart Mill* (Toronto, University Press, 1963–). Both these projects include editions of correspondence.

56. The same author's *Dictionary of Temperance Biography*, briefly describing 382 prominent British teetotallers, 1828–72, was issued as a supplement to the *Bulletin of the Society for the Study of Labour History* in May 1973.

57. For Quaker records elsewhere see *Journal of the Friends' Historical Society*, which includes a 'Notes and Queries' section and abstracts from *Accessions to Repositories* (H.M.S.O.).

58. See G. J. S. Lefevre, Lord Eversley, *Commons, Forests and Footpaths* (Cassell, 1910), and W. H. Williams, *The Commons, Open Spaces and Footpaths Preservation Society: A Short History of the Society and its Work* (The Society, 11 King's Bench Walk, London, E.C.4, 1965: pamphlet).

Chapter 8

1. See below, p. 64.

2. An interesting description of the treatment a family might give to its own collective archives is found in Victoria Glendinning's study of Wilhelmina Seebohm, *A Suppressed Cry: Life and Death of a Quaker Daughter* (Routledge, 1969).

3. An interesting footnote to the history of autograph collecting in the 19th century is provided in an article by C. E. Welch in *Journal of the Society of Archivists*, Vol. 3 (1969), pp. 489–91, about the short-lived Society of Archivists and Autograph Collectors, based on papers of its secretary and founder, Henry Saxe Wyndham.

4. *Publications of the Modern Language Association of America*, Vol. 64 (1949), pp. 319–24.

5. *Manchester Review*, Vol. 11 (1967), pp. 97–120.

6. See, for example, *Business Archives*, No. 30 (June 1969), pp. 24–5, 37; No. 31 (December 1969), pp. 9, 19–23.

7. The Ephemera Society was founded in 1975 to promote interest in this type of material. It publishes a bi-monthly newsletter, *The Ephemerist*.

ADDENDA

Business History

The wealth of material for the labour and social as well as the economic and business historian in deposited records of the Yorkshire woollen textile industry is very clearly shown by Patricia Hudson in *The West Riding Wool Textile Industry. A Catalogue of Business Records from the Sixteenth to the Twentieth Century* (Edington, Pasold Research Fund, 1975).

A survey of the records of the shipbuilding and repairing industry was begun in mid-1976 under the auspices of the Shipbuilders and Repairers National Association and the Business Archives Council.

Periodicals

The Warwick Guide to British Labour Periodicals 1790-1970, ed. R. Harrison and G. Woolven is due to be published by the Harvester Press (Brighton) in 1976.

Religious History

Original Parish Registers in Record Offices and Libraries, Local Population Studies and Cambridge Group for History of Population and Social Structure ([Matlock], 1974).

Visual Sources

The Album of Carte-de-Visite and Cabinet Portrait Photographs 1854-1914, O. Mathews (London, Reedminster Publications, 1974).
The Picture Researcher's Handbook, H. and M. Evans and A. Nelki (Newton Abbot, David & Charles, 1975).

General

COPYRIGHT *see also Museums Association Information Sheet No. 7* on copyright law (2nd ed., revised, 1974).
MUSEUMS *see also The Directory of Museums*, ed. K. Hudson and A. Nicholls (Macmillan, 1975).

INDEX